The
ROAD
To
FREEDOM

LETTING GO OF YOUR BAGGAGE

Peter Allman, M.A.

iUniverse, Inc.
Bloomington

The Road To Freedom
Letting Go Of Your Baggage

iUniverse books may be ordered through booksellers or by contacting:

iUniverse
1663 Liberty Drive
Bloomington, IN 47403
www.iuniverse.com
1-800-Authors (1-800-288-4677)

ISBN: 978-1-4759-4223-1 (sc)
ISBN: 978-1-4759-4224-8 (e)

Printed in the United States of America

iUniverse rev. date: 8/17/2012

For Sara and Nathan

Contents

Introduction

Have you ever tried finding your way through a construction zone in an unfamiliar city? If so, you probably know what it's like to run into dead end after dead end, your GPS navigation system rendered totally useless by the recent road work, your nerves on edge as you thread your way through the heavy traffic. Sometimes life can feel a lot like that. We have an idea of who we want to be—a loving parent, a patient friend, a compassionate person—but at every turn, something seems to get in the way.

I got lost trying to find my way. I made a professional change at age thirty, went back to school, and became a psychotherapist. I had read many books on religion, psychology, and spirituality that helped me let go of a lot of baggage and gain freedom in my life. I met with my minister and other church staff to talk about my questions, decipher my night time dreams, and help me grow in my faith. I married a wonderful woman who is highly interested in physical, emotional, and spiritual health. I surrounded myself with friends who were interested in their psychological and spiritual growth. I joined a writer's group where all the members are interested in my monthly submissions and give excellent feedback.

I came to realize that we all have a human nature and a spiritual nature. I believe our main purpose is to create a divine union, or unite our humanity with our Divine Self. This is what Jesus modeled for us.

Sometimes we live an integrated life. We forgive a friend. We love our neighbor. We pray and meditate. We volunteer at a local non-profit. And then something unexpected happens that sets us back on our journey.

The Divine Self knows the spiritual nature of this human experience. The ego gets us stuck in the human experience and will not allow the divine union to occur. The Divine Self lives in love. The ego lives in fear. The Divine Self lives in the present moment. The ego lives in the pain and glories of the past and the anticipated future. The Divine Self forgives. The ego holds on to grudges.

Paradoxically, we need to fully embrace our human nature while we simultaneously fully embrace our spiritual nature. The purpose in writing this book is to guide you on how to develop a healthy human essence (Section II), help you find your spiritual essence that is already inside of you, and how to create a divine union between the two (Section I).

Each of us needs healthy and functional skills and talents to live in the world. We need to have strengths and abilities to help us meet new people, be successful at our jobs, set boundaries with people, raise children to be self-reliant, learn how to resolve conflicts, and have the communication and coping skills to grow old with our life partners. We need healthy qualities and competencies so we can find fulfilling jobs that match our personality. We need to be skillful and proficient so we can safely co-exist on highways with other cars driving 75 miles per hour. We need to learn these human competencies and evolve into the next developmental stage of embracing our spiritual nature and creating a union between the human and the divine.

This next stage is not adequately talked about or modeled by leaders in the religious or psychology realms. Predominantly, we are taught to live from the ego mind. The ego is simply a way of thinking. It is a mind—a mindset—that is built on unconsciousness and the absence of the Divine. The egoic mind drives us with thoughts of separateness and creates a false sense of self. The egoic mind sees the world in terms of "I want this," or "I don't want this."

This way of living in the world is ruining individuals, families, communities, countries, and our planet. We are taught to perceive our human strengths, abilities, and talents as "mine," which creates an unhealthy persona. By definition, an ego-driven life will be difficult and full of baggage. We will become mired *in* the world. The ego will play all sorts of insidious tricks to keep us disconnected from our divinity—our Divine Self.

Most people think they are living life the correct way because almost everyone else is doing similar things. But this lifestyle falls short and unhappiness is rampant. Alcohol and recreational drug use, abuse of prescription medications, expensive vacations, and galloping consumerism are all methods to try to deal with their malaise. We work hard to try and feel better by putting our self on a pedestal and only take care of our self.

Our egos also judge others, which can harm relationships and ourselves. Our egos have buttons that can be pushed. We get sent to the moon when a spouse, child, or friend says something that triggers intense negative emotions within us. Our egos push us toward the seven deadly sins. Yes, our egos create the thoughts, "I work hard for my money. I will not donate any to (fill in the blank)." Or, "I'm busy and I have a lot to get done. I don't have time to be play with the kids." Or, "The business will never know if I pad my expense account." Or the corporate ego (country) says, "That neighboring country has what we want. We will write policies or send in our military to insure our own stability." And on and on and on.

Our church, synagogue, mosque, or AA group challenges us to name our sins. The spiritual component of our lives knows this is right and necessary. But our egos want us to deny our sins, project them onto others, rationalize them away, or put on a nice smile and thank the pastor/rabbi/priest for a nice sermon and promptly forget everything he or she said.

The ego mind creates unconsciousness and darkness which always leads to pain, suffering, or destruction. This darkness is insidious and dangerously subtle. The ego mind promises us that it will be our friend, take care of us, and make us better than others. But ultimately it will only harm us.

Our Divine Self, which is connected to God/Spirit/Higher Being, doesn't need to glorify itself. Our Divine Self doesn't want us to run on the treadmill that leads nowhere. It wants us to spend more time with the family. The Divine Self wants us to sit and meditate, be in nature, and live a life of abundance. The Spirit wants to guide us to help us grow closer to God. The Divine Self within us wants to help others. The Divine Self wants to create a union with our human essence.

How do we get truly connected to God and our spiritual nature when our ego desperately fights to keep us estranged? First, it is by being an observer of yourself and "seeing" the egocentric thoughts and its wants, desires, and aversions. Then, it is by embracing the Divine Self, the part of us that connects us to our Divine Being's love, universal truths, and specific truths for us.

People of all faiths have a prayer that is similar to "Not my will, but Thy will be done." "My will" equates to the ego. "Thy will" equates to the Divine Self. Jesus said we need to live *in* the world but not be *of* the world. We need human strengths to live "*in* the world." Because we have a great capacity to subvert the will of God to our own, we need to access our Divine Self to be able to "not be *of* the world."

With free will, everyone chooses who or what is running their lives. Since thoughts create our reality, a vital question to answer is: are we choosing thoughts that are from the ego or thoughts from the Divine? Our default mode is the ego so it takes awareness, practice, and discipline to merge into the road to freedom.

The ego is sinister and it has most of us under a spell that has us believe there is a place for ego in one's personality and life. The purpose of this book is to describe a new way of being. Section I of this book defines the Divine Self, the qualities it manifests, and its needed position within your total being. Embracing your Divine Self and creating a divine union with your humanness will bring you closer to God. You will experience happiness, heal yourself, claim abundance, and create the life you were designed to live.

Section II of this book will describe human qualities that we need to be able to live in the world, and how to re-claim them as gifts from God. If these qualities are turned to create an ego, then the three letters of ego will come true: edging God out.

The Buddhists tell us to find our Buddha nature. Christians challenge us to be Christ- like. Jesus said we will do greater things than he. Nelson Mandela quoted Marianne Williamson and said in a speech,

"Our deepest fear is that we are powerful beyond measure. It is our light, not our darkness, that frightens us."

Only by creating strong and functional personality traits, embracing them as God qualities, and tethering them to the Divine Self, will you be able to trust in the inherent goodness of life, awaken to the call of your own higher potential, and live a life full of love and joy. You will not want to be a star, but you will want to be like the three wise men and follow a star.

We do not need to fight with the ego. Rather, we need to focus on growing the light, seeing the Divine in us and all around us, and the ego will automatically get smaller and lose power. Ego will no longer be in the driver's seat. We will have less baggage on our spiritual journey. This is the road to freedom!

Lastly, for many people, the concepts in this book will be new. Many will jump on the learning curve to this new way of being in the world. A word of caution: please do not use this new information to only accumulate knowledge. This will increase the power of your ego mind. Use this information to transform your life. Return home to your true nature and live a life of freedom.

I like my life better when my ego is de-powered and I live with a divine unity. But my mind is in a habit of being driven by the ego. When this occurs, I go back to my spiritual practices and then live a more fulfilled life in this human realm.

Through wise books, friends, and mentors, I have gleaned seven truths that guide my life. When I recorded them, the essence of this book jumped out at me. These truths will be sprinkled throughout all the chapters.

Seven Core Beliefs

(1) We are not human beings that have spiritual experiences. We are truly spiritual beings that are currently having a human experience. Our primary purpose is to create a divine union between our human essence and our spiritual essence.

(2) We need to embrace our humanness and learn skills and qualities to be able to live *in* the world. When believe we own these traits and think these abilities come from our self, we create an ego mind and

will become *of* the world. The road to freedom is to see these talents as Divine qualities and spiritual gifts that we are to manifest and with which we bring benefit to the world.

(3) As stated in the book *Course of Miracles,* there are only two ways of living in the world: in love or in fear. When one lives in a state of love, some of the manifestations of one's life will be joy, forgiveness, acceptance, peace, harmony, and freedom. When one lives in a state of fear, some of the manifestations of one's life will be anger, resentment, jealousy, separateness, and being stuck. The Absolute True state of existence is love.

(4) True reality lies only in the present moment.

(5) Attachment is the cause of all suffering. The release from suffering comes from being non-attached. (Buddha)

(6) Forgiveness and emotional healing are synonymous. If you have created an emotional wound, forgive yourself. If someone else has wounded you, forgive them.

(7) The mind is the chief architect of your life. Everything begins with a thought. Your thoughts create your reality. And, you are not your thoughts.

DIVINE SELF

There is an old story about a peaceful, happy community that lived in a little village. Their ancestors had made a giant statue of Buddha, which was made with gold. The giant golden Buddha was built over many generations by the people. It stood many, many times taller than the tallest person of the village.

The golden Buddha helped everyone who lived in the village. The children were taught that they were like the golden Buddha: wonderful, marvelous, and incredible beings. They were made of love and had all the wisdom of the universe available to them. Through this wisdom and love, they could accomplish anything they wanted.

There came a dark time when distant neighbors, who were not peaceful, sent their army to this village. They did not know what the Buddha represented and only wanted wealth and glory.

The village people were afraid their hostile neighbors would steal the golden Buddha. The village people decided to hide it. Because it was so large, the normal ways to hide it didn't work, so the village people decided to cover it up.

They poured concrete over the golden Buddha, and then rubbed dirt on the concrete to make it look old and filthy. The golden Buddha now looked like an old, dirty concrete statue.

When the army attacked and occupied the town for many generations, they did not pillage the statue because it didn't look valuable at all. After many, many years, the army left and everyone in the village knew the statue as only concrete and grimy.

One day, a villager was meditating by the golden Buddha and when he stood up, he accidentally knocked a chuck of concrete off the statue. He realized there was gold underneath, and the villagers realized the true nature of the Buddha statue.

We have covered our true nature, which is our Divine Self, with an ego that gets stuck in the past and future. We have covered our true nature with an ego that is only concerned with identity and the successes and failures that accompany it. We have covered our true nature with busyness, attachments, and judgments. This creates a lot of baggage and keeps us stuck in life. We lose our freedom.

At the core of our being is a Divine Self. This is our spiritual heart and is our timeless essence. It has no affiliations or ties to the thoughts, ideas, and habits of our mind. It is the source of peace, happiness, compassion, and joy. It works ceaselessly to reveal itself to us, but our busy mind—our ego—opposes it.

The Divine Self is the source of light and life within us. This light will help us see the illusions of attachments, desires, and cravings created by the ego. These all keep us unhappy and stuck in life. This light will help us see the cause of our suffering and move us toward freedom.

Most of us cover up our true nature—our Divine Self—by external dynamics. Like the gold Buddha was defined by the external concrete and dirt in an attempt to protect it from marauders, we define our self by accomplishments, what we wear, where we live, who we know, where we travel, the size of our bank accounts, our body shape and size, and what culture dictates is "in" and "out."

When we live defined by externals, we lose access to our essence, our soul, and the ability to truly know our Divine Self and God. This creates a fear-based life because externals are always changing. When we are not connected to our spiritual ballast, the ego will always need to be shored up.

A good metaphor to help us understand the Divine Self is an ocean. When we look at an expansive ocean from the shore, we see many waves. We might describe them as big, small, powerful, weak, high, or low. These terms make sense when describing a wave, but make no sense when applied to the ocean.

The waves are manifestations of the moon's gravitational pull on the waters of the ocean. These waves are ever changing. They rise and then they fall. They might appear near to us or far away. The waves are part of the ocean but we know they are not the ocean.

Our thoughts and behaviors are like the waves of the ocean because of the gravitational pull of the ego. As a wave rises in the ocean, we will "rise" and play many roles; businessperson, parent, volunteer, or Christian. When we identify with the "wave" we will live in our humanness and lose the connection to our Divine Self, lose our source of love, and move in and out of being fearful. To deal with this, we will try to build our self up and further boost our ego. When we look deeply into our self and realize we are an ocean of a Divine Self, the fears will vanish. When we live from the Divine Self the "waves" will appear but we know they are manifestations of our thoughts and behaviors. We will reside and find our foundation from a bottomless source of love, and a greater intelligence than ours. We will more likely live the prayer, "Thy will be done."

> # YOU DO NOT NEED TO SEARCH OUTSIDE OF YOURSELF OR ACCOMPLISH ANYTHING TO BE IN TOUCH WITH YOUR DIVINE SELF.

You do not need to search outside of yourself or accomplish anything to be in touch with your Divine Self. All you need to do is let go of the external concrete and dust, and let go of the ego's pull. You don't need to get in a car, fight traffic, or try to get a parking spot. All you need to do is take the journey inward. Physicist Stephen Hawking said, "… humans are an adventurous species." Take the ultimate adventure. Look inside and bring to the light the dark thoughts and hurtful memories from the ego mind. By definition they will lose power and you will be more conscious of your thoughts that guide your life decisions. You will then have the ability to more fully embrace your spiritual nature and be guided by the goodness of God.

Paradoxically, the journey inward is the journey forward. Bring to the light your God- given talents, strengths, and the never-ending source of love that wants to be manifested in the world.

Who we really are is consciousness and energy that is way bigger than our life situations, problems, interactions, meetings, and endeavors. The Divine Self is formless, timeless, and eternal. When we are connected to our true nature and live in the present moment, we respond to the world with a wisdom that comes through us and from a state of love. Sadly, most of us forget about our divine heritage and get lost in our humanness—our ego. We are as God created us; we are love and have a natural affinity for life.

When you uncover and find your true golden nature, you will live from an ocean of wisdom, courage, clarity, charity, happiness, and love. You will successfully live *in* the world, but not be *of* it. This is the road to freedom!

CHAPTER ONE

Your Greatest Strength is Your Greatest Weakness

You believe you are doing well *in* the world. You are successful at work and/or at home. Your human strengths are creating an income, children who are involved in many activities, and you are well liked by your peer group. You are taking the bull by the horns. You are the captain of your own ship. You are pulling yourself up by the boot straps. You are climbing the ladder of success. You are going to be a millionaire by the time you are (fill in the blank). Or, as Leonardo DiCaprio's character yelled at the bow of the Titanic, "I am king of the world!"

Living only from one's human strengths is like the Titanic. It might look big, shiny, and impressive. But it is destined to sink. Living only from our humanness and not including the spiritual realm is beyond short-sighted—it is the recipe for disaster because the ego mind is captain of your ship. You are becoming *of* the world.

Webster defines ego as "The self especially as contrasted with another self or the world." When you live your life by this definition, it will sooner than later lead to the second definition of ego in The World Book Dictionary: "conceit." And, remember from the Introduction, ego could stand for edging God out.

When you see yourself separate from others, nature, and the world, you are more likely to be self-centered, see life as a win-lose paradigm, and treat others poorly or as a commodity. You will live a life of scarcity and you will fight to acquire the perceived limited resources in interpersonal relationships and in the world. Living from this worldly position will lead to a never ending search to fill a self-created void.

The ego sets up a mental world where you are separate, scarcity abounds, others are out to take what you want, and fear rules your life. The ego has no substance so it creates identities of credentials, self-image, self-worth, possessions, or anything else that creates hierarchy and separateness. As a consequence, we live in a bad dream and forget who we really are.

A great example of this is the man who is experiencing a middle age crisis. His identity of where he works, husband, and father are insufficient for his happiness. He then tries to find happiness in the world; a younger woman, a new car, and a new lifestyle. Sadly, this ego-driven person hurts others and will inevitably find himself existentially unhappy again.

Ego is an accumulation of a habitual configuration of thinking and lifestyle patterns. Section II describes the format for human behavior is Think-Feel-Act; every thought creates a feeling, which lead us to act in certain ways. The habitual and conditioned thoughts, feelings, and behaviors create the ego existence. They are configured around an identity, and the sense of self.

Even though it is simple to define and describe ego, paradoxically it is not easy to disentangle from its power. If a person is oblivious to his ego, narcissistic behaviors will occur which drive others away. This further empowers the ego thoughts of fear, separateness, and scarcity.

The great psychologist Abraham Maslow created the theory of the hierarchy of needs. He said we first need our physiological needs of hunger, thirst, sleep, and other drives to be fulfilled. Then we need to feel safe. We need to feel secure and avoid pain, fear, and anxiety. Then we need to have a sense of belonging. We need affection, intimacy and to have roots in family and peer groups. Then we can look at esteem needs: self-respect, feeling we have adequate competence, and fulfilling achievements. He then claimed that less than one percent of people reach the last stage called self-actualization. This is when a person grows to his or her full potential, is independent of culture, discriminates between the means and the ends, and has peak experiences.

Maslow said there are two levels of self-actualizers. First, there are people who are "merely self-actualizers" or healthy. These people have healthy strengths, have learned to be helpful to others, and live by the golden rule. They love their family and raise children who are self-reliant and contribute to society.

Then there are self-actualizers who are spiritual in orientation and have frequent peak experiences. They identify with universal human values, such as love, forgiveness, and freedom. They live a life of service to others, joy, and bliss. They can stand against the crowd.

People who have developed healthy human strengths and are "merely" self-actualizers typically do well in their culture. Yet they still are not happy without external successes, trips, material accumulations, and others giving them compliments. They are still tied to the human realm. Their thoughts are usually centered around "*my* will be done."

Merely being self actualized doesn't make one free. To live a life of freedom, one has to use human strengths while connected and tethered to one's spark of divinity, one's Divine Self. This section of the book will fully describe this process and give strategies on how to live the prayer "Thy will be done."

At the end of each chapter, I have created an Action Plan with three recommended exercises. They are not assignments. I know that every exercise will not resonate with you. The point is to use this new information from each chapter to help transform your life—not to merely accumulate more knowledge. So practice one of the items, two, all three, or come up with new ones that are better for you. Good luck!

CHAPTER TWO

Being

We are human beings. We are not human doings.

What is being? How does it compare to our ego? Being is formless. It is timeless. Being is eternal. It is spiritual. Being is a state of consciousness, a state of awareness. It is our connection to God. Jesus said the Kingdom of God lies within us. It resides in our being. It is your Divine Self.

Our culture has limited means for talking about our core being— our Divine Self. It is not honored, thus we have incomplete and restricted language to describe this part of our life. Our culture prizes and accentuates the doing part of us, which gives this piece a strong framework and abundant language.

For example, when you greet someone, you probably ask, "How are you doing?" A typical response is, "Busy." This elicits in you the response of "I'm busy too." You both respond, "Busy," which means "I'm following the correct life script of our culture so please accept me." The initial question infers that our *being* is not important and what we *do* is paramount. This social interaction then goes one step further. If what we do is so important, then we better do a lot of it. This song-and-dance is usually followed by pleasantries and both people depart feeling accepted by others but disconnected from their being.

One of the typical questions asked when you meet someone new is, "What do you do?" A dad might ask his child at the dinner table, "What did you do today?" Or a spouse may ask her husband, "When will you get to the Things To Do list?" All of these questions communicate that you better be doing something or you will be judged or evaluated in a negative manner.

The World Book dictionary defines being as "a state or condition of fully realized potentialities; end point of the process of becoming." In contrast, our body is form which is impermanent, changing, and becoming more or less. In the end of our life, our body will die. Our being is formless, timeless, and unchanging. Our being—our Divine Self—has been and always will be.

The way we were created and designed to live in the world is to be connected to our being. From this union and relationship comes the strength of identity; knowing ourselves, embracing our gifts and talents, helping ourselves and others, and being connected to our Higher Being. Meditating, praying, journaling, interpreting nighttime dreams, participating in fellowship groups, being in therapy, being in nature, talking honestly with trusted friends, are all ways to be connected to our essence—our being.

Ideally, from our being comes our doing. When we know ourselves, we will find the right job that fits our personality. We will participate in extracurricular activities that energize us. We will surround ourselves with good people. We will be aware of the calling to do kind acts and help non-profits. We will probably do things that are outside our comfort zone.

From our doing and earning an income comes our having. We need to have a roof over our heads. We need to have food. We need to have clothes. We want to have some of the latest electronic items and bestseller books. Some want to have a family and take vacations.

It is a be-do-have progression. Our culture (our corporate ego) has completely flip-flopped this truth. We have been taught and modeled that we are measured by what we have. We think to have worth we need to have the latest fashions, the bigger house, the latest gadgets, the fancier cars. This is the American dream. If a neighbor has a country club or athletic club membership, we feel we need to have it. To accomplish all these things, we must do the work and earn the money. So we do, do, and do. Sometimes we work two jobs. Both parents work to maintain a standard of living. Our credit cards are maxed out so we need to do more. We push our children to do activities so they can keep up with other children. We have them doing dance, soccer, music lessons, and other organized activities. We do not let them be in the neighborhood with friends. They must do a structured activity.

Our culture has created a model of have-do-be. If we *have* things, and *do* the right things, then we will *be* somebody. Anyone who reads this will see the folly in this paradigm. Yet most people in our culture follow it blindly. The "have" and the "do" are solely stressed at the expense of the "be." The ego defines itself by what it has and what it does. It is not connected to being.

The Spirit resides in our being. Galatians 5; 23-23 states, "…the fruit of the Spirit is love, joy, peace, patience, kindness, goodness, faithfulness, gentleness, self-control…" Our culture does have language on how to manifest these fruits. Be loving. Be joyful. Be peaceful. Be patient. Be kind. Be good. Be faithful. Be gentle. Be in control of yourself.

If we are *being* patient with our children, we will *do* better parenting, and then *have* better adjusted children. If we are *being* kind to our spouse, we will *do* behaviors that are important to him or her, and then *have* a better marriage. If we are *being* good to co-workers, we will *do* helpful behaviors, and then *have* a happier and better workplace. If we are connected to our Divine Self, our human strengths can be used to create goodness.

God's gift to us is our being. It takes awareness to be connected to our being. Awareness comes from consciously reducing the amount of doing in our days, and slowing down our busy minds. We need to create time each day to quiet our minds and break the habit of incessant thinking that leads to habitual doing. One way to do this is through meditation, which is described in detail in Chapter Seven.

Many Christians have used the strategy of asking the question "What would Jesus do?" in an attempt to more fully live their faith. This strategy will only create short term changes in a person because it is dealing with the *do* part of the progression. If the question aimed for the foundation and tried to create long term change, it would be: "How do I manifest Jesus' being?" From the *being* would then come the *doing* which would de-power the ego and create a life that was fully human *and* fully divine.

If we continue to lead busy lives, we will not meditate and slow our minds. Then, our thoughts and actions will keep us distant and disconnected from our being. They block the natural magnetic pull towards God. Sri Sathya Sai Baba, a spiritual leader from southern India said, "When the magnet does not attract the needle, the fault lies in the dirt that covers up the needle." Meditation will slowly clean the "dirt" and allow our being to be attracted toward what Jesuit priest Anthony de Mello coined, the "Eternal Magnet."

From a quiet mind, we can be intentional about our doing. We will be able to manifest formless (thoughts) into form (actions). From this quiet space, the Spirit will express love, joy, and peace. It takes awareness and effort to manifest the fruits in the material world. With practice, we will be patient while we parent our children. We will be kind while we are driving. We will be joyful when another person accomplishes something. We will be loving to all whom cross our paths.

Identifying with work and material goods are ways our ego keeps us disconnected from our being. When most of our time, thoughts, and energy are directed toward what we do and what we have, there is little time left for connecting to our being. In the movie Fight Club, Brad Pitt's character Tyler Durden attempts to break people of this insidious way of living. He pulls a young, underemployed retail clerk out of a store and holds a gun to his head. He asks him over and over what his life dreams are. To help him wake up, Tyler states, "You're not your job. You're not how much money you have in the bank. You're not the car you drive. You're not the contents of your wallet." Tyler said he would come back later to make sure the clerk was following his life dream.

Sometimes it takes a "gun to our head" to wake us up. Many people who have experienced a life threatening illness realize that working countless hours and owning the biggest and latest toys are not important. Being with the ones you love and sharing yourself with others are essential to living a fulfilling life.

The ability to be with your self is the key. This will entail the ability to be comfortable with silence. Silence will reveal yourself to you. Be mindful with what crosses your mind. Be a highly interested observer of yourself. Don't seek anything. Observe. Watch. Be awake to your life. Don't judge things as "good" or "bad." If you want to change something in your life, change it. Slowly you will get re-connected to your being. You will realize the kingdom of God lies within you. You will be. This is the road to freedom!

Action Plan

1. Select a fruit of the Spirit and practice *being* that each day.
2. Live today like you've got one month left to live.
3. Discern what is the "dirt" that is stopping you from being more fully drawn to the "Eternal Magnet." Gently, start sweeping away the dirt.

CHAPTER THREE

How we experience "I"

Most adults play many roles in their lives. A woman may do the work expected of a mom, spouse, part-time employee at a local business, volunteer at a non-profit, coach of her daughter's soccer team, and deacon for her church. A man may do the same as a dad, spouse, vice-president of a bank, disciplinarian, bus driver for his children, and member of a civic club. Which role(s) is the real you? Which of these doings comes from your true being?

It is all too common for a person to live in the realm of "I am what I can do." Since a person does the work of a parent, employee, and volunteer, an answer to the above questions could be; "All those roles are me! I am a spouse. I am a mom. I am a volunteer. I am a part-time employee." But something about this is lacking. This is a list of qualities; a similar list could also be attributed to a house—it is a two story, brick, attached garage, with a renovated kitchen. It doesn't fully resonate that all those roles are the totality of you. There is a deeper, spiritual essence within you.

I challenge you to do an exercise: list ten roles you played in the last week. Another way of stating this is to list ten different experiences of "I" you have had in the last week. The roles—the "I" experiences—could be as simple as "grocery shopper" and "driver," and as significant as "son," "husband," and "spouse," and any hobby or activity like, "photographer," or "tennis player." Then spend some time with the list and choose the one(s) that you feel are the real you.

Linda is a forty year old woman who is married, has two children, volunteers at her children's elementary school, and has a sister who is her best friend.

Linda participated in this exercise. Her list of "ten different experiences of "I" are listed below:

1. driver of car
2. volunteer at school
3. mother
4. sister
5. wife
6. daughter
7. disciplinarian
8. garage sale shopper
9. sewer of clothes
10. cook

Linda had a difficult time identifying the "I" experiences that she felt were her real self. She finally listed mother, sister, and wife.

I asked Linda a series of questions to help her "peel away the different layers of the onion" and find her Divine Self. The first question I asked Linda was why she listed those three roles. She answered that she felt she didn't have to wear any masks when she was a sister, mother, or spouse.

I followed up with the question of why she didn't have to wear any masks. She answered because she felt safe. I asked why she felt safe. She thought for a moment and said, "Because they accept me for who I am."

I asked, "Who are you—what state are you in—when you are with them and feel safe?" This question was more difficult for Linda to answer. She finally said, "I feel I can care for them and they care for me."

I asked another question to peel off one more layer of the onion. "What's going on in those relationships for you to be able to care for them and for them to care for you?" Linda squirmed in her chair and gave me a look. She looked down, deep in thought. About sixty seconds later she said, "I'm devoted to them. I want what's best for them."

I gave her a reassuring look and asked a compounded question that summed up her previous answers: "When you are having the experience of being a mother, sister, and spouse, why do you feel safe and don't have to wear any masks, why do you feel accepted for who you are, why do you feel cared for and want to care for them, and why are you devoted to them?" Linda exhaled and said, "Because I love them and they love me."

Linda became aware that her being—her Divine Self—is a state of love.

Did you arrive at a similar answer? What state are you in while performing these roles that make you feel they are the true you? Is it because you are *being* more caring, *being* more creative, *being* more in a state of love? If so, is the True You—your being—found in the acts of empathy, the acts of creativity, the acts of love?

Our sense of "I"—which is our ego—is a subjective identity. From this exercise, you can see there is a never-ending succession of transitory "I's." The ego is always changing, impermanent, and partial. Ego experiences are non-enduring and, if our human essence is not connected to the Divine Self, life is a mundane reality where we are always seeking distractions. But the ego believes itself to be absolute, permanent, and whole. It wants us to believe it is the only game in town and thus, should be more powerful.

Our Divine Self—our being—is timeless and eternal. It is that divine spark from God. The Buddhists call it one's Buddha nature. Christians refer to it as Christ consciousness or being Christ-like. The Quakers see it as the Inner Light. The Hindus define it as nirvana. It is all the same thing expressed in different words.

Ego is tied into form and needs to have an identity separate from others. A person's ego might state, "I am an American." "I am a Christian." "I am a hard-working person." These statements could be judgmental to people who are not similar. For example, judgments could be made of a person you meet from France. "I am French," can stir up, "You didn't help my country in the war in Iraq." "You must not be a strong Christian because I read where church attendance is weak in France." And, "Why do people in France close down their shops for two hours over the lunch hour? You are probably a little lazy."

These judgmental thoughts create a wedge between you and the other person. You might feel a little anger which doesn't allow you to fully *be* with this person. You might feel superior which further distances you from the other person. There is little chance for the gifts of the Spirit to be manifested in this interaction or future interactions.

How does this fit with the identity of being a Christian? Obviously, it doesn't. If this person's Christian identity is stuck at the ego level, he will be stuck in his humanness and not fully love the other person. If he has embraced both his human self and his Divine Self, he will more naturally accept the Frenchman. He might want to ask him about his two hour lunch break to learn more about how to relax and *be* with your food and lunch guests. He might be able to *be* with another person who has a different political view. He might grow and be more tolerant of others. He might be able to love thy neighbor.

Psychologist Carl Jung said the ego is full of distortions and projections. Through awareness and meditation, these problems can be dissolved and a clearer picture of reality can appear. You can "see" the negative, judgmental thoughts as a product of your own mind. You can "see" that old biases still have power and you can gently set them aside. You can "see" old messages that your parents taught, and start to reprogram your thoughts to create more loving life scripts.

The process of creating a divine union between your human essence and spiritual essence will enlarge your picture of every situation. To return to the example I used above, his divine union could state, "I am a citizen of this world who happens to live in America." This will broaden his picture and include the Frenchman as a fellow citizen. Instead of seeing his work ethic as single-mindedly positive, it broadened his view to a paradoxical perspective. "One of my strengths *and* weaknesses is my hard work ethic. There might be some benefits from taking a longer lunch break. I may die of a heart attack if I don't learn how to relax."

Expanding his religion from a label to a way of life could create a new perspective with the Frenchman. "I am a spiritual being who was raised Christian. I am going to practice living my faith, and not judge him but love him." The Buddha said, "It is not good reciting the scriptures if you don't live your life by them. It is better to know a few texts well, to overcome desire and live your life properly. This will give you a wonderful life." Expanding the circle of acceptance and more fully loving his French neighbor will create a more wonderful life.

Even "I am a kind person," can keep you stuck in your ego. The motivation behind kind acts is everything. If your motivation is to foster an identity of a kind person, your ego will want recognition. Scorekeeping will ensue. Tit-for-tat giving will be the norm. The ego will want to be rewarded and appreciated. Separateness and judgment will rule and everyone will be hurt. Your spiritual growth will be stagnant.

True kindness comes from your being. The motivation of an act of kindness comes from an internal knowing of what is the right thing to do. There is no means to an end. Desire for anything in return isn't expected. These acts of kindness are from the Spirit, not from the ego. "Ambition and anger will disappear when you stop concerning yourself with the fruits of your actions," is a quote from an early Sanskrit Buddhist text.

The Divine Self has a natural affinity for life and knows it is connected to nature, others, and God. If judgment and anger are directed outward, they will come back and harm the source. The Divine Self knows we are made in the image of God. Since God creates from a state of love, so does the Divine Self. The Divine Self is forever watchful. It knows when the ego gets bruised and wants to assert its power. Gently, the Divine Self doesn't resist the situation, but loves self and others, and helps resolve the life issue. This is freedom!

All spiritual masters know who they are not—they know they are not their egos. The egoic "I" comes from the attachment of thoughts, feelings, memories, activities, accomplishments, and body. "I" depends on what others think. This leads you to thirst for approval. You will try to control others and situations so they will think positively of you. You will react negatively when others don't respond the way you think they should.

You will realize how flimsy the "I" is when you try to navigate through the "thems." By realizing you are not your memories, thoughts, feelings, and what you do; you will more likely to be connected to your Divine Self. You will more fully realize "what you sow, so shall ye reap." You will more likely get outside of yourself and help others. This, of course, will help you. This is the road to freedom.

Action Plan

1. Live an "I" experience in a state of love.
2. Let go of a religious label and replace it with living the messages of the religion.
3. If your ego gets bruised, don't resist the situation but love the other person and try to resolve the situation.

CHAPTER FOUR

Moving From Judgment to Discernment

Semantics is important when trying to understand these two words. One of the ways Webster's dictionary defines judgment is, "a formal utterance of an authoritative opinion." Encyclopedia dictionary defines discernment as, "The act or process of exhibiting keen insight...coming to understand something clearly and distinctly."

The word judgment connotes authority, power and defense of one's position. Discernment signifies seeing into a situation and making a decision that is healthy and functional for a person at a specific time. When people are judging, they see the situation as right or wrong. They see outcomes as good or bad. When people are discerning, they are saying yes or no to the situation.

The situations in which one can judge or discern range from the simple to the complex.

Let's start with a simple situation that is trivial and over-the-top, yet hopefully makes the point. You are writing a letter and you drop your pen on the floor. You might think something like, "You idiot. I can't believe you did something so stupid." This is an emotional response based on judgment.

Is it right or wrong that you dropped the pen? Seriously, spend a moment contemplating this question. Is it right or wrong or something else?

If you answered "right," the following mental chatter might occur.

"Fantastic, I dropped the pen on the floor. I'm glad I did that." This response doesn't resonate.

If you answered "wrong," you might think or state, "You idiot. I can't believe you did something so stupid." This answer doesn't feel good.

Most of us judge our behavior and answer the question, "It was *wrong* I dropped the pen." We have personal beliefs about how we should act and not act in the world. If the behavior does not match the personal belief, we tend to respond with overly intense feelings, which are called emotional responses. For example, we believe we should be able to do something as elementary as hold a pen. "You dim wit," you say to yourself with anger. "I hope no one saw me do such an asinine thing." We also have generally agreed upon social paradigms about how things should be in the world. When our behaviors do not match these social norms, negative and judgmental thoughts ensue. "That was very dumb of me. Get your act together!"

Judgments are evaluative and ego driven. The ego is only concerned about how situations and interactions impact it. The ego always wants to look good and get what it wants from the world. If something doesn't go according to plan, the ego will judge it as "wrong" or "bad" because of its negative effect. The ego will resist, which paradoxically, makes the problem persist.

There is another response to dropping your pen. You can experience it without judgment. The reaction is to think, "It just is." You dropped your pen. It's on the floor. It has happened. There is no taking it back. It just is. Pick it up and move on. This is the process of discernment.

This simple example shows that emotional responses are created when we judge. We see how silly it is to experience the emotions of happiness and elation when we judge the dropping of the pen to be right. Hopefully, we also see how silly it is to experience the emotions of anger, stupidity, and embarrassment because we dropped the pen.

Emotional responses are more intense messages to mundane events and make situations cloudier and messier. Emotional responses amplify and make the situation more severe. In contrast, feelings give you important information which helps in discerning the situation and making clearer decisions.

Feelings are part of the human experience. Feelings are from the heart and are internal messengers that help with the discernment process. Judgment-emotional response and discernment-feeling are two kinds of feedback loops. This first loop can amplify the situation and make it even more difficult to resolve. The second can clarify the situation and give you the needed information to make healthy, functional decisions.

For example, you feel anxious when you wake up in the morning. Is the anxiety a feeling or an emotional response? If it is a feeling, you will be able to discern the message from the feeling of anxiety. Maybe the feeling is telling you that you need to review some notes before work. Or you need to resolve a conflict with someone. Once the issue is resolved, the feeling disappears. If it is an emotional response, the anxiety will be too overwhelming, you won't be able to pin-point the source of the anxiety to a specific factor, and the anxiety will continue.

The ego constantly judges people, conditions, and outcomes because it is only concerned about itself. The ego is evaluating every situation and is interested in how people and circumstances are impacting it.

Our human strengths tethered to the Divine Self constantly discerns what to do in each life circumstance and situation. The Divine Self is concerned with making wise choices where the end never justifies the means and the goal is to create win-win outcomes.

Discernment means you recognize, comprehend, and understand the situation. You are becoming more conscious, which means you are becoming more aware of your thoughts and feelings. "I have anxiety this morning," the discerning mind states. "I need to go over my notes again before the meeting at work." You study, edit, and become better prepared.

Figuring out your life lesson within each experience is also part of the discernment process. For example, "I don't want to wake up being anxious, so I want to better prepare for meetings the day before," is a discerning thought that will help reduce the feelings of anxiety.

Let's up the ante with another example. You're driving the speed limit trying to get to a meeting. The street light turns yellow. What is your thinking process? The ego wants to judge the situation as wrong. "How dare the stupid light turn yellow on me. Now I'm going to be late! I don't have any luck." You slam the brakes in an emotional state of anger.

The human strengths tethered to the Divine Self sees the street light turn yellow and quickly discerns whether to continue or stop. You realize you are too far back from the intersection and you stop the car. You know there is nothing personal in the street light changing yellow. You stay in the present moment and make a resolution that you will arise earlier in the morning so you won't be late to any more meetings.

Let's raise the ante a little more. The principal calls because your child hit another child at school. If you judge the situation, your ego will get twanged. Your judgment could be at yourself, your child, the principal, or a combination of the three. "What have I done wrong? I'm going to be viewed as a horrible parent." Emotional responses of anxiety and fear will follow on your drive to the school. Or, "My child is bad. I'm going to ground him until the end of the year." You will carry the emotions of anger and hostility into the meeting. Or you could fire up both the negative judgments of your parenting skills and your perspective of your child. This will double the unhelpfulness you bring into the meeting. Your clarity and good problem solving skills will be left behind at the curb.

In this example, the initial part of the process of discernment is to ask the principal if both children are okay. When that is accomplished, the process continues at the principal's office where you help figure out the consequence for your child. You might ask the school counselor to help your child learn better coping strategies. You separate the behavior from the child and know your child is not bad, but his behavior was not appropriate.

The discernment process continues when you, or you and your spouse determine the consequence at home. You continue to discern if your child is learning better coping strategies. And you discern whether your child shows remorse and help him deal with that feeling.

The paradigm of "It just is," is a state of acceptance. You did drop the pen. The light did turn yellow. Your child did hit another child. They are facts. They are objectively true. They are not going to change. Acceptance does not mean you should not do anything. You need to discern if you can improve upon what is. This is the Serenity Prayer: "God grant me the serenity to accept the things I cannot change; courage to change the things I can; and wisdom to know the difference."

You can improve the way you hold the pen so you won't keep

dropping it. You can leave a little earlier in the morning so if the lights turn yellow, you won't be late to the meetings. You can teach your child coping strategies so he is less likely to hit more children.

Sadly, there are more complex situations that occur in life. For example, your daughter gets raped or your son gets seriously injured by a drunk driver. Are these situations right or wrong? It is easy to judge these as wrong because our loved ones have been deeply harmed. If you judge these situations, you might get stuck in an emotional response of hatred of the other person. The overall negativity of the situation will not allow the process of forgiveness and will impede you from fully being there for your child.

A healthier and more evolved perspective would be to discern what your child needs in each and every moment. If you are caught up in hating the perpetrator, you might lose opportunities to love your child. If you're more concerned about judging the acts, you are less likely to discern the life-giving measures your child needs. If you are stuck in the past and not started the process of forgiving, you will not know what to do in the present moment, or how to look ahead to future needs.

These situations are very dark and incredibly difficult. One can easily get mired in multiple judgments and emotional responses. It takes a sword of discernment to cut through the negativity to help find a place of love where you can see clearly what is yours to do. This lucid state will only occur if you paradoxically let go so you can be with your child in the midst of the carnage This is when forgiveness begins.

The process of discernment allows actions to follow which will benefit others.

One mom discerned the need for tougher drinking and driving laws. She created MADD, Mothers Against Drunk Drivers, and they helped change laws in all fifty states.

Parents have asked university personnel to make campuses safer for their daughters. Parents have lobbied lawmakers and educated social workers and police to make the sexual assault examination process and gathering of evidence more humane.

Thoughts are like boomerangs. Matthew 7:1 states, "Judge not, that you be not judged. For with the judgment you pronounce you will be judged and the measure you give will be the measure you get back." The Divine Self knows everything is interconnected so if judgments of hatred and negativity are emitted by the ego, that is exactly what will come back. This karmic reaction will keep a mom in a mental prison and she will not be able to fully help her daughter. If the father wants to kill the drunk driver for maiming his son, he will live in a state of loathing which will keep him from fully loving his son.

The 13th century mystic poet Rumi wrote, "Out beyond ideas of wrong doing and right doing there is a field. I'll meet you there." This is a state of being that is free of judgments and comparisons. It is a place of acceptance and non-resistance. Before you meet others in this field, you need to first meet yourself there. When you stop judging yourself, you will more easily refrain from judging others. That is a field of enlightened consciousness. This is the road to freedom!

Action Plan

1. I will watch my ego to see when it judges a situation.
2. If you find yourself in a dark place, let go of judgments and negative thoughts.
3. Stop resisting a negative situation in your life. Let go, discern what is yours to do, and take new actions.

CHAPTER FIVE

Empty or Full (of oneself)

Edward Glen Osten enters a mall and immediately sees a mom with three children. A mad, crying baby is in a stroller throwing her bottle and doll on the floor. The three year old is crying and trying to break away from mom's firm grip. The five year old has wandered away and is looking in a toy store window. Mom is yelling his name to come back.

Edward judges the mom for allowing the situation to get out of hand. He quickens his pace to get past the chaos. He sees the men's clothing store, mutters something derogatory about his wife who didn't get his shirts to the drycleaners in a timely manner. He feels inconvenienced because he now has to purchase two oxford cloth shirts on his way to the airport. He doesn't notice that the two crying children are now quiet.

Grace Olivia Dolan enters the same mall a minute after Edward. She is there on her lunch break because she offered to buy a gift for her boss with the pooled money for Boss's Day. Grace sees the frantic and overwhelmed mom. She immediately kneels down and picks up the doll and bottle and playfully returns them to the baby. Grace looks at the three year old and says, "I bet you've only got ten steps to the door. Why don't you count them with your mom?" The toddler's tantrum is broken and he looks up at his mom. Grace asks the mom if she can get her third child and walk him back to her. The mom smiles and says "yes."

Edward and Grace were both on a tight time schedule. Both could have felt trapped by their moments in the mall. The difference is Edward is attached to his ego which means he's so full of himself that there is no room for another. Grace practices spiritual disciplines that allow her to be aware of her ego's cravings and aversions. She empties herself of these thoughts which allow her to be open to God's will and help others.

There are many reasons Edward is trapped in his ego. One of the reasons is because Edward is caught up in his identities. He thinks he is a very important businessman. That identity gives birth to embracing the thought that his self-worth is tied into his net worth. Because he has made lots of money, he believes his identity is more valuable than that of others. He expects others to take care of his "trivial" needs so he can take care of the more "important" ones. Being a perfectionist is another one of Edward's identities. He thinks he has to be perfect in his appearance and job performance. He then projects this perfectionism onto the mother in the mall who is clearly in a situation that is not perfect. He is so full of himself that it splatters onto others.

We know from Chapter Three that our identities are subjective, transitory, impermanent, and partial. The ego thinks they are absolute, permanent, and whole. Edward is imprisoned in his identities, which creates much suffering in his life and others.

The ego has a sly solution to the problem of the illusionary nature of identities. The ego creates masks that we put on which makes the identities feel real. For example, during a sales presentation, Edward dons the mask of a competent, charismatic, and caring person. At the office where he manages eight people, he dons the mask of an authoritarian boss, worker-bee, and one who has an air of superiority. At home he figured out this manager's mask did not work, so he dons the mask of an aloof, unhappy dad, and spouse. Paradoxically, he wears a happy mask when he's in the public with his family. Unconsciously wearing a mask is the antithesis of the Divine Self.

Grace meditates everyday to quiet her busy mind. She sits in a quiet place in her home and she watches her thoughts. She lets go of them soon after they appear. Grace is highly interested in what arises in her mind, but is an unattached observer. After much practice, Grace reaches times when she empties her mind of thoughts.

Grace knows she is not her thoughts. Thoughts are just thoughts. They are not who we are. When ideas or worries about work arise, she is unafraid and open to them. She notices them as a third party observer.

Grace knows she is not her job. When she starts to re-play a delightful experience, she watches it impersonally and practices returning to silence. She is not that experience. These are things that she does, but it is not her being.

We get lost in the past and the future while we live in our head. The ego gets fed by the gloating of the past and dreading of the future. The ego attaches to past injuries and future wants. No wonder people feel overwhelmed. They are carrying around the past and the future while they are trying to handle the present.

The Divine Self lives in the present moment unencumbered by the thoughts of the past or the future. The Divine Self is awake, aware, and able to respond to every new situation out of a state of love.

A good strategy to stay in the present moment is to return to your senses. Feel your body in the chair. Feel the wind, the warmth or coolness of the environment. Feel your hands on the steering wheel of your car. Hear the birds in the trees. Smell the freshly cut grass or smoke from a chimney. The mental chatter will subside. You will feel more alive, and know more fully what action needs to be taken.

Suzuki Roshi wrote a book titled *Zen Mind, Beginner's Mind*. His premise is that we need to be like a small child who lives totally in the present moment. The child is full of curiosity, wonder, and amazement in whatever crosses her path. We should not have a full mind of preconceived ideas, judgments, and expectations. Beginner's mind is present, unfettered, and ready to observe things as they are.

The beginner's mind does not resist what happens. It is open to whatever occurs. It is curious and investigative. An adult's mind full of expectations resists all the time. "That car should not have pulled in front of me." Unless you want to suffer, why would you resist this? It *is* in front of you. It *is* your reality. "Damn it, my friend should have called me by now." Your friend has not called. If you want to talk to her, please call her. Unless you want to suffer, do not resist what is. In a mind full of preconceived ideas and judgments, resistance will occur, which causes suffering. A beginner's mind is open, accepting, and observes things as they are. In acceptance there is peace and freedom.

We all like to be the one that knows—the answer, the idea, the person. But when that happens, we do not have a beginner's mind and we are not open to new possibilities. We feel disappointed and resentful when experiences don't happen as our busy and cluttered mind thinks they should.

We are more likely to find our value from within when we have an empty mind. When we look for value in the world of possessions, we will have a cluttered mind. Yes, the newly acquired item will bring us short-term happiness. But the material item will become out of style. It will break, or we will lose interest in it. So we will look for another material good to provide happiness. But it is the nature of pleasure to not be sustainable.

A Buddhist story tells us there was a wise Zen master whose counsel people from far and near would seek. One day an important businessman from a large city came to visit the master. "I have come today to ask you to teach me about Zen. Open my mind to enlightenment," he commanded.

The Zen master smiled and said that they should discuss the matter over a cup of tea. When the tea was served the master poured his visitor a cup. He poured and he poured and the tea rose to the rim and began to spill over the table and finally onto the clothes of the wealthy man. Finally the visitor shouted, "Enough. You're spilling the tea all over. Can't you see the cup is full?'

The master stopped pouring and smiled at his guest. "You are like this tea cup, so full that nothing more can be added. Come back to me when the cup is empty. Come back to me with an empty mind."

If you're full of yourself, there is no room for God. Freedom comes when you empty yourself and get out of the way. Then, and only then, is there room for God. Being empty, paradoxically, you will be full of the Spirit. Be empty, open, highly interested, and ready. Your Divine Self will then be connected to your Higher Being. Then you can move mountains. This is the road to freedom.

Action Plan

1. Pick a situation and enter into it with a beginner's mind.
2. Try practicing staying in the present moment for thirty minutes.
3. Write about an experience where you felt free and you and God were working together.

CHAPTER SIX

The space of awareness

Since I have been practicing meditation I now experience a space where I become more aware of my thoughts and feelings. I "see" the judging, busyness, and all the "I's" that manifest in my world. The thoughts of these life circumstances arise and, with awareness, they dissipate. Initially, the power of the thoughts and feelings are strong because I associate them with me. When I watch them in a non-personal manner, I realize they are not me...they are just thoughts. With an awareness that is deeply interested, unafraid, and open, the power diminishes. I even find humor in the negative energy I gave to the situations. I find freedom in this space of awareness where my Divine Self resides.

I practice living in this space of awareness. Many life circumstances try to jar me out of this state of freedom. For example, I'm driving the speed limit and a person pulls out in front of me and drives eight miles an hour slower than I am. I'm in a hurry because I'm behind on my things-to-do list (Chapter Two). My subjective identity (Chapter Three) of an important person arises, and I judge (Chapter Four) the slow driver as a dolt. I am full of myself (Chapter Five) and I'm an angry person. My ego is driving me—and wants me to honk my horn and tailgate him.

I become aware I am gripping the steering wheel of my car. I slowly breathe in and consciously exhale. This helps me come back to the present moment. I want to let go of the anger so I continue the meditative practice of breathing. Slowly I find the space of awareness and I "see" the absurdity of my reactions.

My Divine Self is now in the driver's seat and my ego incrementally loses power to the point it is no longer in the "car." My human strengths of healthy decision making, switching lanes, and defensive driving are being utilized. I am still aware of the street, the car in front of me, the street light, and all other pertinent material items. I am driving in a peaceful manner and making healthy decisions on a busy street.

The inner space of awareness has created freedom from my ego. My happiness is no longer dependent on the car in front of me. I have traveled home to my Divine Self which is the spiritual dimension. This space allows me to not get stuck in life circumstances, let go of negative thoughts and feelings, and find purpose and meaning in life.

Since I'm new to this practice, my ego tries to get back in the "car" and still speaks loudly from the passenger seat. It states, "Can you believe what that guy is doing to you?! When you pass him make sure you give him a dirty look. Even better, cut him off when you merge back in his lane. You need to teach him a lesson."

I practice staying in the open space of awareness. I am fully conscious of my ego's voice. I don't judge it or resist it. I try to find humor in its diatribe and let go of its desires. Only by bringing that voice to the light can I be aware of it, stay centered in my Divine Self, and practice being non-attached to my ego. Paradoxically, I still accomplish my things-to-do list. *And,* I do it in a more authentic manner. The work doesn't feel like work. I am both engaged and carefree. There is a natural flow and the outcomes are win-win. Customers and co-workers feel better and I find meaning in each experience.

A great practice to disarm the ego is to realize that nothing is personal. If Steve, your boss, is flying off the handle, that is Steve being Steve. It is not personal to you. If your friend Susie is not asking about you and going on and on about her life, that is Susie being Susie. It is nothing personal to you. And really, who else can Steve be but Steve? If you expect another boss to show up, you are full of delusions.

Another example occurred many years ago. My wife, a friend of ours, and I founded a non-profit after school program for teens who are at-risk for many unhealthy behaviors. We named the program Lighthouse and I was responsible for finding a facility. I drove around the area of town where we wanted to be located looking for "For Sale" signs. Every house or store front did not meet our needs. I asked a real estate agent to help me find a facility. She and I looked at many properties. Some locations might have worked, but the neighborhood association did not want us to run a program for teens who are at-risk in their neighborhood. I read the newspaper looking for properties for sale or rent. I came up empty handed every week.

It had been a month of searching and I was unsuccessful finding a facility. Notice the pronoun: *I* was working hard. *I* was responsible for securing a property. *I* was driving around looking for "For Sale" signs.

I vividly remember a Friday afternoon around 4:30. The real estate agent and I had spent the afternoon looking at houses. Afterwards, I drove around by myself hoping to find a place. I had nothing to show for thirty days of diligent searching and hard work. I was mad at God because I felt forsaken and lost. I was at the end of my rope, and I said out loud in my car to God, "I have felt all along that this project was yours. The feedback from the community and listening to my inner voice has been positive. If you want Lighthouse to open and help teens, you find us a facility. I will still be a faithful servant, but I'm letting go and putting this in your lap."

Two days later in church, a gentleman commented that he knew I was looking for a facility for our program. I nodded my head. He asked if I had looked at a certain property. I told him I had not. He gave me the name of the owner and suggested I check it out.

I made an appointment on Monday, and by the end of the week we had signed a rental agreement and we soon moved into our new facility.

My ego works hard to stay in power and feel important. I need to be an observer and see it. When I was in my car and sternly spoke my mind to God, I was letting go of my ego. By allowing a divine union to occur, I was re-connected to God and the natural flow of life.

Only at that point was I consciously living "Thy will be done." Before my state of despair and anger in my car, *I* was in charge. *I* had to make it happen. In my defense, this is what most of us have been taught and modeled. My motivation was not egotistical or self-centered. My motivation was drawn from my Calvinistic work ethic; "If you want something done, you better do it yourself." This is still an ego driven life because I was not connected to my Divine Self.

What these two examples illuminate is that the Divine Self is consciousness. It is the state of being conscious of one's thoughts, feelings, and one's existence as a spiritual being who is having a human experience (1st of the Seven Core Beliefs.) It is formless, timeless, eternal, a state of love that has a natural affinity for life. Only by meditating and quieting the mind, can one experience the present moment, be watchful, and from an awakened consciousness, respond to the world from a state of love.

> **ONLY BY MEDITATING AND QUIETING THE MIND, CAN ONE EXPERIENCE THE PRESENT MOMENT, BE WATCHFUL, AND FROM AN AWAKENED CONSCIOUSNESS, RESPOND TO THE WORLD FROM A STATE OF LOVE.**

The term Buddha means The Awakened One. Buddha was fully conscious. There is a wonderful story of Buddha walking on a country road. A peasant saw Buddha and exclaimed, "You are the Lord." Buddha responded, "No I'm not." The peasant said, "Well then you are the Messiah." Buddha responded, "No I'm not." The peasant then said, "Then you must be a God." Buddha responded, "No I'm not." The peasant was frustrated and asked, "Well then who are you?" Buddha responded, "I'm awake."

Buddha came to the awareness that he was not his thoughts, feelings, and knee-jerk responses to life circumstances. He unmasked this lie and taught this great discovery for forty-five years. Jesus made many references to the old must die. He stated, "You must be born again." These are references to transcending an old way of living (ego) and shifting to a way of life (divine union) that is substantially and significantly bigger.

A wonderful metaphor to help practice letting go of the ego and living in the Divine Self is to be like a leaf on a river. Each person is a unique leaf on his or her own unique river. Each river has its own person-specific bends, deep and shallow areas, reeds, and rocks. The current of the river is the flow of life that each person needs to learn how to trust. Sometimes the leaf gets entangled in the reeds or hits a rock. If a person judges the "rocks" he might continue to bash into it, swear at it, and stay stuck hitting the rock. If a person "sees" the rock, discerns the flow of the river and slowly gets back in the current, he will suffer less and move on with his life.

The ego lives in the past and the future. The ego wants to know what lies beyond the bend in the river. The ego will create emotional responses of anxiety or anger if the river doesn't go in a known direction. The Divine Self trusts God, trusts the river, and knows goodness will prevail. The Divine Self will utilize human strengths to help navigate the new direction. The Divine Self will lean into the prayer, "Thy will be done," and ask God for help and a stronger faith. With these practices, the leaf will continue flowing with the river. With these practices, we will continue to be aware, trust, move from fear into love, and humbly follow God's will and the Divine Plan that is implanted in our Divine Self.

This final example comes from another Lighthouse experience. After seventeen years, we had outgrown our current facility. Our board of directors wanted to run a capital campaign to build a bigger facility. I agreed with the decision and I knew it would be a tremendous amount of work. I practiced being a leaf on the river and went with the flow.

This time I practiced being led by my Divine Self and my human strengths were put to work on many specific duties. Grants were written, brochures were printed, sales calls were made, the Home Builders Association agreed to help, three lots were purchased, an architect selected, and a building design was approved by the board.

Nine months past and I was working hard. Again, notice the pronoun; *I* was working hard. Half of the money was raised for the capital campaign and no new prospects were in sight. The campaign had hit a dead end. In hindsight, I had quit being a leaf on the river and *I* had taken back the responsibility of raising all the money and crossing the finish line. My motivation wasn't bad. I had gone back to what I knew; work hard, be responsible, and make things happen.

I distinctly remember the moment when I consciously made a decision to de-power my ego, be more fully conscious of my Divine Self, and get reconnected to my Higher Power. I was at the mailbox hoping for pledge cards and donations. I opened the mailbox and only bills were in it.

In frustration, I made a conscious decision to become a leaf on the river. I prayed to my God, "This is your project. It has always been your project. I have been a faithful servant. But I have taken the control of the campaign. It is back in your hands. I will continue to work for its success, but the sole responsibility no longer rests on my shoulders. You lead the campaign, you bring the donors, and you bring the right people."

Soon after, a board member found a highly competent person to coordinate the various campaigns of the capital campaign. I shared the status of the campaign with a key person in the building community and he formed a committee to call on businesses to volunteer their services. The campaign took on a life of its own. My efforts were more from a flow experience instead of the drudgery of before.

I have many human strengths which are rewarded in society. I have a personality which people like. But I had become imprisoned within my own ego and personality. It had got me half way through a $1.7 million capital campaign. But only half way. Being aware of this made me more awake to my dilemma. I was then able to step out of the way and allow God's will to unfold...with many people's strengths working for the common good.

Become aware of your mode of existence in all interactions. Monitor yourself during business meetings, luncheons, dinner with your family, golf with your buddies, play days with your children, running into friends at the grocery store. If you are more concerned with yourself than the relationship, you need to ask yourself some questions. Am I too much in a "go mode" to *be* with the others (Chapter Two)? Am I too much into myself and not interested in the others (Chapter Three)? Am I judging this interaction instead of discerning what is mine to do (Chapter Four)? Am I so full of myself that I can't allow other points of view into the conversation (Chapter Five)? Am I experiencing emotional responses (Chapter Four)?

Creating a space of awareness is a practice. Sometimes our humanness takes over and we find ourselves in an ego state. During coffee with a friend, you might find yourself waiting for your turn to talk instead of really listening. You might feel offended by something they said, when in reality, what they said was not meant to be personal to you. You might judge a decision your friend made, shut down emotionally and then not be there for her.

It's easier to see this in others. For example, politicians get caught in their egos by bowing to special interest money, thinking of how a decision will only affect their state, or purposefully voting against a bill because it will harm the other political party. If the politicians lived from their Divine Self, the interest of our nation and other nations would drive their decisions. Political affiliation would take second place to sound legislative bills. Military power would give way to diplomacy and helpful foreign policy.

We all need to create a space of awareness and live a Divine Life where we utilize our human strengths to create a better world. We will miss the mark and find our ego leading us. We need to find the humor in the situation, and gently de-power and let go of the ego, and be led by our Divine Self. This is road to freedom!

Action Plan

1. If you feel like something is personal, create a space of awareness and realize that nothing is personal and "Susie is being Susie."
2. If you feel stuck somewhere in your life, let go of it, so you can give it to God, while you continue to discern what is yours to do.
3. Name a "rock" that is in your "river." Start today to not judge the rock, and discern what strategies you need to employ to get around it.

CHAPTER SEVEN

Meditation

One of the quirky acts on the Ed Sullivan show in the late 1960's was a man who spun plates on top of long, wooden poles. He would start spinning one plate, pick up another plate and spin it on top of a second pole. He would continue to do this until eight plates were spinning on eight different poles.

The performer had to be constantly aware of the plates he spun earlier because they would lose speed and wobble. He would run back and re-spin them so the plates wouldn't fall and break.

The audience loved watching the man run back and forth trying to maintain the velocity of the first, second, and third plates, while he started spinning the seventh and eighth plates.

The performer was on constant alert and had to move all the time to be successful. There was tension in the air and the audience would applaud for his four minutes of frantically dealing with spinning plates and the accompanying anxiety.

Our untrained minds tend to be like this performer. The mind creates a thought and it spins around and around. Then the mind creates another thought. We believe this thought to be important and we spin it around too. This continues and when the eighth thought comes and seven other thoughts are still spinning around, we find ourselves anxious and stressed.

The ego pushes us to live this way. The ego dwells in the past and the future—that's why most of our thoughts reside there. The ego prides itself on creating an identity of being busy—that's why we continue the rat race. A ploy of the ego is to have us look outside our self so we lose access to our inner being.

Alan is a forty-five year old who is married with two children. He works as a manager for a national organization. One morning, he is in his bathroom getting ready for work. While he's shaving he has a thought; "I need to push Ron harder so he signs more sales contracts this week." This thought creates a second thought; "Next week is the end of the quarter and I know my boss will e-mail me about the importance of a good bottom-line." This creates a third thought; "How am I going to *spin* the report to make it look good?" The fourth thought comes "If sales were better, it would be easier to have a positive report."

Alan comes down for breakfast with his wife and children. The eight year old child blurts out, "Dad, come see my art project." The ten year old says, "Dad, can we play catch tonight?"

Alan is lost in his thoughts that come from his ego identity of manager. He goes back to spin the first thought because he can't let it drop. "I need to put the fear of God in Ron because he's the weak link."

"Dad, I hand in the art project today. Come see it!"

"Dad, you didn't answer me about playing catch tonight."

Alan's wife breaks his internal plate spinning and says, "Alan, your children are talking to you."

"Kids, I'm late for work. I've got to run," Alan says while grabbing his coat.

Alan misses many important moments in his life because he has too many "plates" spinning in his head at once. Since most people in our culture live their lives the same way, they don't know there is another option. As Henry David Thoreau said, they "live lives of quiet desperation." Sadly, this is the attempt of the ego to feel important, but it ultimately set us up for failure.

In fact, if Alan experiences a moment of silence, he becomes uncomfortable and starts spinning plates....because that is what he knows. It is a habit.

The only time Alan quiets his mind is when he focuses on a woodworking project or when he plays racquetball with a friend. In both of these activities, his mind is focused on one thing. This stops the mind from spinning more plates. Once the game or woodworking project ends, Alan's mind soon goes back to the habit of creating thoughts upon thoughts upon thoughts.

Meditation is a way to see all the thoughts—the plates—and gradually understand that they are only thoughts. If one wants to have a more peaceful life, one can let the thoughts go and come back to the present moment.

"Be still and know I am God," is written in Psalm 46. Only a mind that does not have multiple plates spinning can know and fully experience God. Let's take a word or two away from this verse and see what happens;

Be still and know I am.

Be still and know.

Be still.

Be.

Reverse the plate experience. Take plates off the poles. It is easy and peaceful to spin one plate. When you are finished with a thought—one plate—let the thought go and *be* with your environment until you need to spin another plate. Then let that thought go. The most amazing thing will happen. People will come up to you and remark that you are different. They will ask you why you are in such a good mood. They will want to *be* with you.

On the spiritual journey, it always gets back to our being (Chapter Two). Our culture is completely dominated by doing at the expense of our being. Stillness is essential for the spiritual life. A line from the Tao te ching speaks of this; "Returning to the root is silence. Silence is returning to being."

You may have heard the old quote, "Silence is golden." The next line that is rarely cited is, "Speech is silver." Speech—the doing—is ranked second to silence. Silence—the being—is ranked first.

There are many different ways to meditate. There are hundreds of books on meditation. In this chapter I offer a brief tutorial on a method that quiets the mind, so one can "Be still"…and be.

It is important to start meditation by sitting somewhere with your back straight and both feet on the ground. If you have been practicing meditation for a while, you might sit in a full lotus body posture. If you are new to the practice, you can sit in a chair or sofa with a pillow at your back to help you keep your back straight The mind can only be one place at a time. You're either thinking of this or that. Now, the "this" and "that" flick back and forth quicker than a flea, but the mind can only be one place at a time. Since we want to train our mind to be still, we must focus our mind on one positive and neutralizing thing.

While you are sitting, practice focusing on, and be aware of, each breath that comes in through your nostrils and out through your nostrils. Breathe from your stomach. When you inhale, let your stomach out. When you exhale, your stomach will relax inward. In time, and with more awareness, you will start to feel the coolness in and warmth out. The mind must have something to occupy it—give it only one thing—your breath.

A discursive thought will enter while you are practicing being aware of your breath. That's okay. The goal is to watch your thoughts in an unattached manner. Picture a river and the current taking the thoughts away from you. Keep going back to your awareness of each breath; breathe in and breathe out. You will soon become more present. The thoughts about the past and the future will fade. You will become more whole because your thoughts won't be about your scattered "I" experiences (Chapter Three).

Another thought will appear. Watch the thought in an impersonal manner. Let the thought go while you re-gain awareness of your breath. This practice takes the untrained, undisciplined, everyday mind and creates the development of bare attention. This is a single-minded awareness of each and every thought. This practice is to simply observe the mind, and the feelings it creates. Have a deep interest in this process of watching your thoughts. Be unattached and impartial to each and every thought. Simply resting in an open, unafraid state creates awareness and a peace that is beyond understanding.

When you practice meditation, your thoughts will begin to slow down. The space of awareness (Chapter Six) will become larger and larger. You will live your life more in a state of mindfulness and awareness of your divine presence. When your child wants to show you a piece of art, you will *be* there with him. When your wife wants to process an issue, you will *be* there with her.

There is an old and famous Zen saying, "When I eat, I eat. When I sleep, I sleep." When you practice having your thoughts stay in the present moment (4th of the Seven Core Beliefs), when you eat, you will be much more aware of the taste of the food. When you walk, you will be much more aware of the sounds of nature, the wind on your face, touching the ground, and muscle movement. When you play catch with your child, you will be there completely with him. If another "plate" starts spinning, become aware of it and gently let it go.

"Silence is the great revelation," wrote 6th century B.C. Chinese philosopher Lao-tse. With the practice of meditation, we will "see" the discursive thoughts which will reveal much about us. With silence we can see what thoughts arise more than others. Do we have more thoughts about work, family, health, or relationships? What does this say about our attachment to our different identities? What conflict do we need to resolve? Where do we need to forgive?

Paradoxically, as your awareness of these thoughts improves, your silence will deepen. As you become more comfortable with silence, your ego will be de-powered and your Divine Self will be empowered. For that time period, you are on the road to freedom!

The mind is the chief architect of our reality. If you are in a positive mood, your thoughts created that state. If you are in a negative mood, your thoughts created that state. (This is not true if a person is experiencing clinical depression, anxiety, or other major mental health disorders.) Joy, peace, happiness, content, and calm are all created by your thoughts. Anxiety, despair, frenzy, agitation, and anger are all created by your thoughts. You have to first be aware of your thoughts that create these states of being. Then you need to know that you can let go of the thoughts. It is counter intuitive, but welcome your thoughts for the purpose of letting them go.

You are not your thoughts (7th of the Seven Core Belief) They are just thoughts. If you are not your thoughts, what are you? You are not a human being that has spiritual experiences. You are a spiritual being who is currently having a human experience (1st of the Seven Core Beliefs). You are a being of love that wants to experience many things on this earth and share God's love in everything you encounter. If you are lost in your thoughts, you will not be aware of the Universe guiding you to what is best for you. There is an old saying that God first whispers to us. If we do not hear, God speaks a little bit louder. If we still don't hear, God causes a noisier and more noticeable event in our life so we take time to stop what we're doing. If we still don't hear, we will experience an even louder and more obvious event. The motivation for each of these communications is for the benefit of us and others.

Please stop spinning so many plates. Meditate and quiet your mind. Life doesn't have to be so hard. Be still and know God. This is the road to freedom!

Action Plan

1. For a fifteen minute period, practice staying in the present moment. When your thoughts drift to the past or future, be gentle with yourself, and come back to the present moment.
2. While you are driving or doing an activity at home, turn off the radio or television and *be* with whatever you are *doing*. Or, truly *be* with another person
3. Watch your thoughts as a detached observer. Practice this long enough to realize thoughts are just thoughts—you are not your thoughts.

CHAPTER EIGHT

The garden of Eden and the garden of Ego

Genesis 2:15 states, "The Lord God took the man and put him in the garden of Eden to till it and keep it." This is an example from "Being" (Chapter Two) where from Adam's *being* comes his *doing*, which produces his *having*.

The garden of Eden can be seen as a metaphor for a state of being where God's love is forever present, the basic necessities of life are abundant, and humanity lives together peacefully. It's perfect in its beauty and sustenance. Humans share a true love relationship with God.

Adam and Eve did not feel separate from God and nature. Because of this they did not have a need to create separate "I" experiences (Chapter Three). When they toiled, they toiled. When they rested, they rested. They lived in the present moment and did not judge anything as wrong or bad (Chapter Four).

They were divinely one with everything. They were not full of themselves (Chapter Five) because they were full of God's love.

Does this sound like the divine union between one's human nature and spiritual nature?

This state of innocence was broken when the serpent enticed Eve to eat from the tree of knowledge of good and evil. The serpent told Eve, "…when you eat of it your eyes will be opened, and you will be like God, knowing good and evil."

Adam and Eve ate the fruit, and the ego started to emerge. These three letters—e g o—could stand for edging God out. Their egos began to edge God out of their lives. From the book of Genesis, immediately (after their fall from grace), Adam and Eve knew—because they were self-conscious of their differences—that they were naked. They "...hid themselves from the presence of the Lord God." Adam said, "...I was afraid..." Since that time, we have followed Adam and Eve out of the garden of Eden and toiled in the garden of Ego.

A Buddhist precept is pain is inevitable, suffering is optional. Pain is unavoidable. As a human being, you will experience physical and emotional pain. If you learn your lesson, forgive yourself and others, and then let go of the experience, you will not suffer. Suffering is the main manifestation of living in the garden of Ego. This occurs because we see ourselves as separate and have lost our connection with God. We have replaced it with materialism, seeking pleasures, and trying to avoid pain. We identify with what we own. We identify with our children's accomplishments. We identify with our jobs and our income. We look outside for truth and validity.

As we all know, this does not bring lasting peace or happiness. But we continue to play this game because we experience temporary happiness. When happiness wears off, our egos tell us to try to find similar experiences. We fall into the trap of being busy: working hard so we can own these possessions which bring us short term pleasure. Sadly, many people die still grasping for the ultimate vacation, and paying off their credit cards, in a futile effort to find lasting happiness.

Some people let go of the senseless consumerism and take the journey back home to their Divine Self. They give up trying to prevail in the garden of Ego and instead, learn their life lessons, forgive, let go of their earthly attachments, and take the "road less traveled." Part of their motivation to leave the garden of Ego is they feel isolated, trapped, and they are tired of suffering. They re-enter the metaphorical garden of Eden wiser, knowing that happiness comes from being interdependent with God, nature, and others.

In the movie Star Wars, Luke Skywalker is an apprentice to the wise Jedi knight, Obi-Wan Kenobe. Luke, like all of us, is lost in his ego and is overly influenced by the culture of his day. Obi-Wan is trying to teach young Luke the ways of the Force. Luke is more interested in the advanced technology of his culture and his own mis-perceived fighting strengths. A dramatic moment is when Luke is flying his fighter ship into a small canal on the Death Star in hopes of firing a blast down a narrow shaft to destroy it. Luke and his flying partners are totally focused on the feedback of the computers and their analysis of the data. Obi-Wan tells Luke to use the Force. Realizing that he won't be successful if he relies on his own devices, Luke takes off his headset and disengages the computer. After a moment of quieting his mind, Luke finds clarity and fires a blast that makes a direct hit.

Luke Skywalker trained and developed his human strengths. Luke also learned to trust the Force by practicing spiritual disciplines. Through the mentoring of Yoda and Obi-Wan, he de-powered his ego and got connected to his Divine Self (the Force). Through pain and crises he opted for growth and change.

We all must leave the garden of Eden. We must develop human strengths so we can live "in the world." There are few in the fields of psychology, religion, and formal education who are teaching us anything else. There are few Yodas and Obi-Wans. We are trapped in a culture that models only ego development and feeding the ego through, among other things, consumerism. We become "of the world."

When we dis-empower our ego and connect to our Divine Self, we are more open to an intuitive knowing which occurs when we live in harmony with the Divine. When we quiet our mind and the internal static, we are more receptive to energy, intelligence, and consciousness outside ourselves. When we realize we are part of God, we more easily live the prayer, "Thy will be done."

The absolute first step to dis-empower your ego is to meditate (Chapter Seven). You must be able to quiet your mind and "see" your thoughts. Once this occurs, you will create a space of awareness (Chapter Six) where you will be able to more closely examine your day-to-day mind. For example, the observing mind will know the thought, "I'm a bad parent because I over reacted to my child not cleaning his room," is not true. The observing mind will discern that you acted in a way that was inappropriate, but you are not a bad parent. The observing mind will "see" that negative mental activity as just thoughts, and let the thoughts go.

You will then move into your being—which is a state of love—and communicate to your child. From love comes forgiveness: you will tell your child you are sorry for your behavior. From love comes discernment: you will tell your child about possible consequences and what needs to be done. You will more easily separate the person from the behavior. You tell your child you love him and his behavior needs to change. You will also love yourself and practice changing your behavior in the future.

In these examples, your ego wanted to be in the dominant position in your life and not rely on God or others for help. Your ego would have taken on the "I" (Chapter Three) of "bad parent."

When your mind is quiet, you will be more likely to be connected to God in your internal and external worlds. The internal static will be replaced with intelligence greater than yourself. You will more likely "know" the right thing to say. You will more likely "know" the best decision to make. Even though the rational mind is telling you one thing, the mind connected to the Divine will "know" that the counter-intuitive decision is the healthiest choice.

Externally, your quiet mind will notice what Carl Jung coined synchronistic events. These are life circumstances that are beyond our understanding and for our betterment. For example, you go to a store and run into an old friend. She tells you something that you needed to hear for your personal or professional growth. You did not call her and cause the interaction. It is provided to you by intelligence way greater than yours. Many people call these interactions or events a "God thing."

When we live from the Divine Self, we open up to allow life to unfold. We are more resilient to deal with whatever happens. We don't resist life. We accept everything is the way it is supposed to be. We are not lazy or laissez-faire. We are fully awake and know there is work to be done. We use our strengths wisely and do what is ours to do. Work is more an effortless effort.

By viewing life as abundant, we make possible the journey back home to our Divine Self. We return to love, joy, safety, and forgiveness. We return in a state of maturity, knowing the union with our Divine Self is by grace and our internal yearnings. We walk by faith, trust in God, and have reverence for nature, others, and our self. This is the road to freedom.

Action Plan

1. Forgive yourself or someone so you can merge onto the road to freedom which takes you to the Garden of Eden.
2. Be awake, alert, and ever watchful for synchronistic events in your life. Expect them in a non-attached manner.
3. Let go of the thoughts that you are poor or you want to be super rich. Claim the middle way of abundance: you will always have what you need.

CHAPTER NINE

How to Get Unstuck and Be Free

Robert, a successful salesman, had reached the top of his professional field. He was an esteemed member of his community, and was making very good money. He had an outgoing personality, worked hard, and hated conflict so he tried to be everybody's friend.

These strengths at work were weaknesses at home. He was estranged from his wife. She spent outside their financial means and they never resolved marital issues. He was angry at his sixteen year old son who quit high school football and wanted to hang out with his girlfriend.

These negative family dynamics led him to gather at his country club's 19th hole bar and drink after work. A driving under the influence ticket landed him in my counseling office.

I asked him who he was emotionally close to. "It sure isn't my son any more. If my dad told me I had to stay on the football team, I would have stayed on for fear of my life," he answered. "I don't know what is the matter with today's youth. They text, e-mail, Facebook, and never actually talk anymore. I haven't really talked to my son in over two years."

"Who do you talk to?" I asked him.

"Used to be my wife. But all she does is nag…and spend money."

"It sounds like you're angry."

"Hell yes, I'm angry."

"How do you express your anger?" I asked him.

"I don't express it because I'm afraid my son will never talk to me again. I don't express it to my wife because I don't want another fight. So I brood on it all night long and I act passive aggressively."

I asked Robert how a toddler shows his anger. He quickly replied, "By throwing a tantrum." I asked why he didn't throw a tantrum. He responded because he didn't want to act like a child. He then added, "So I stuff it."

I asked the Dr. Phil question; "How's that working for you?"

He smiled and said, "Not very well."

"I'm sorry you're stuck," I responded from the heart.

A mother came into counseling to talk about her fourteen year old son who was diagnosed with Asperger's Syndrome. This is a mild form of autism which manifests in people with low social skills, obsessing on certain thoughts, anger, and over-sensitivity to a variety of stimuli.

Connie was an extremely bright, motivated, and loving person. She had turned her world upside down to try and help her son. The symptoms continued despite her best efforts.

She wanted to learn ways to work harder to help her son, and learn about any latest research on Aspergers. Her face was ashen white, with deep circles under her eyes.

I complimented her on the successes of keeping her child mainstreamed in the public schools. I complimented her on her great parenting skills. I complimented her on the support group she created for other parents.

I then reflected to her, "This is the first time in your life you have been brought to your knees. Your human strengths have helped your child immensely, but now you are stuck. Your son's special needs have stopped you on your path. You are doing the only thing you know—to keep using your strengths to help your son. But somehow that is not enough."

Tears welled up in her eyes. She nodded and grabbed the Kleenex box.

We all get stuck in life. A wonderful metaphor to illuminate this is a river. Each person is in a canoe or boat on his or her own unique river. Sometimes the river is deep. Sometimes it's shallow. Sometimes the current is fast and sometimes it's slow. The river bends to the right and then to the left. And, in every person's river there are rocks and boulders. When we run into a boulder, our tendency is to blame the boulder, and complain to the universe that it shouldn't be there. Sometimes we keep ramming into the boulder expecting a different result.

Freedom occurs when we trust the current of the river, maneuver back and around the boulder, and continue on with our journey.

One thing we can be sure of in life is there will be more boulders farther down the river. If we don't resist this fact, we will be more conscious, observe what is happening on the river, and then effectively communicate with the people on our boat, or individually maneuver around without hitting the boulder.

Our ego demands to be in control, so when there is a bend in the river and one cannot see the state of the river, the ego judges, worries, and becomes fearful. A person who is connected to his Divine Self knows that with God's help, everything can be dealt with. The state of the river after the bend might not be our preference, but one knows "this too shall pass," and soon the current will take the boat in another direction.

Robert had many "boulders" in his life that he kept ramming in to. He, like most of us, did not communicate effectively with his family members. He expected them to read his mind and he was afraid of conflict. He stopped helping his wife around the house because he had been keeping score for years. On his tally sheet, he had more marks than his wife. He was stuck in his ego.

In Connie's perception, her "boulder" was so big it covered the width of the river. There was no way around the boulder even though she put her best efforts into the problem. Even though her motivations were good and loving, she was stuck.

There is another thing we can be sure of in life: the boulder never dams the river. There is always space in which to get past the obstacle.

Connie was attached to the hope of her son having a normal life. Her motivations were loving, but her "normal" was too small. I shared with Connie that there are some university professors who have Asperger's Syndrome. I asked Connie if she ever had unique and quirky professors—the ones who got lost in their work, didn't maintain much eye contact, and were extremely bright in their disciplines. Connie did remember such professors and smiled. We talked about researchers and lab technicians who can engage with one subject for hours upon hours, are other good areas of employment. Soon she found hope that her child could live successfully in the world. She started to let go of her attachment of a "normal" life and trusted more in God that her son will be able to live in the world.

A toddler does not have sophisticated human strengths and coping strategies. When a toddler is mad, he is mad and throws a tantrum. When a toddler is sad, she is sad and cries. Adults have learned elaborate coping strategies to be more "mature" and not show their true feelings. Many times these strategies are basically unhealthy. Anger gets stuffed and then later explodes at an innocent third person. Sadness gets denied and grows into depression.

Freedom is the ability to cry when you're sad. Freedom is the ability to talk about what angers you and work on resolving the conflict. Freedom is allowing yourself to be happy and sing in the shower or dance to the music while you're cooking in the kitchen. Freedom is letting go and trusting the Divine.

A toddler will instantly let you know if he is in pain. Hunger, fear, fatigue, or a scrape on an arm will be communicated loudly and quickly. Once the toddler communicates and the need is taken care of, the child does not hang on to the painful experience. The child does not come back later that week, and say "Mom, I am still mad at you because you served lunch thirty minutes late which really made me hungry." The child has moved on and is living in the present moment.

Many adults have painful experiences in which they have used defense mechanisms to hide awareness of the pain. Robert's dad never showed him love and Robert is unaware of his need to fill that void which keeps him stuck in life. He had tried to win approval of his wife and children by working hard and earning money. Connie's younger sister died at a young age, and Connie is unaware of her fear of life and death. This keeps Connie stuck and unable to trust that the future will be okay for her and her child.

Freedom is being acutely and painfully aware of hurtful experiences, forgiving self and others, communicating to a trusted person about that pain, and practicing strategies in the present moment so healing can occur.

The ego lives in the past and the future. If people's thoughts reside here, they will be stuck because the only time to create a healthy life is the present moment. Many adults consciously and unconsciously hang on to old experiences and then live the life of a martyr, orphan, wounded child, athletic star, prince, princess, or many other identities that keep them stuck in life.

The ego is a black hole. The ego always has you believe that who you are is not enough. Since the ego is built on identity, can a "salesman" or "mother," "athlete," or "altruist" ever be enough? Isn't there always a better salesman? Isn't there always a better way to mother? Isn't there always a faster runner, or better tennis player? Isn't there someone who gives more of herself or gives more money? Isn't there always a more popular or richer prince or princess? These thoughts drain our life force and keep us stuck.

Freedom is living in the present moment and being awake to what is. Freedom is not judging the present circumstance, but observing your likes and dislikes. If you resist an experience that you dislike, you will suffer and become stuck. If you accept the experience—like the boulder in the river—you will communicate, set boundaries, or use other coping strategies to stay in a state of freedom. If you keep drawing a bigger and bigger circle of acceptance, you will live in a more constant state of freedom. We are free when we accept what is.

Freedom is slowing down, connecting to your being which is timeless. Once you are in touch with your being, wisdom evolves which helps you decide the next step on your journey. You will find that there is a fire in your belly. You will have passion for your work and be connected to the eternal flame of God.

Freedom is knowing your values which will guide you in the world. One core value is forgiveness. This is the antithesis of how the ego operates. The ego is all about the self and needs to maintain separateness from others. When you hold on to a grudge, you have separated yourself from the other person. The Divine Self knows you are one with everything and forgiveness gets you re-connected to that unity. Forgiveness heals.

Another core value is service to others. This is also an antithesis to how the ego operates. The ego is all about self—not others. The ego might give to another, but its reason is to get something in return. The Divine Self wants to feed the hungry, clothe the naked, and visit the elderly or people who are imprisoned. The Divine Self also knows the paradox:

"In giving you receive" is true because of our interconnectedness. This creates win-win outcomes because it feels good to do good.

Freedom is also having faith in something more than you. By definition that will get you beyond your ego, because the ego is all about self. A faith in a Higher Being acknowledges a power which is greater than you. De-powering one's ego and actually letting go of the ego creates a real connection with the Divine indwelling –the Holy Spirit. It is actually making a union with the Divine and the human—like Jesus. Yes, we can live a life like Jesus when we live with a divine union.

This may seem like daring language and very arrogant. But when one surrenders one's ego and lives connected to the Divine—as Jesus did—paradoxically there is intense humility because one knows it is from God's grace. It is not earned. Living from the Divine Self is a conscious choice and the peace and love that flow from it are a gift.

Being humble will de-power the ego and create freedom in one's life. The word humble comes from the Latin word humilis, which means lowly, on the ground, of the earth. The word humus comes from the same root word. Humus is the material produced by the slow decomposition of plant and animal matter and forms the organic portion of soil. From this rich composition comes new growth.

The same process occurs with humility. When we slowly decompose our ego, this will form a divine union which will create new growth in our lives, guided by the Holy Spirit. The fruits of the Spirit will more naturally flow from us.

This paradigm is rarely reinforced in our culture. In fact, authentic humility is not often understood. The Dalai Lama wrote, "It is important to distinguish between genuine humility, which is a type of modesty, and a lack of confidence. They are not the same thing at all, although many confuse them. This may explain, in part, why today humility is often thought of as a weakness, rather than as an indication of inner strength, especially in the context of business and professional life."

John Wooden, the famous basketball coach of the UCLA Bruins, said, "Talent is God given. Be humble. Fame is man-given. Be grateful. Conceit is self-given. Be careful." Many people live life not being humble, grateful, or careful. When this occurs, usually the ego runs rampant, there is no connection to the Divine Self and pride is manifested.

Pride goeth before a fall is a common adage. The true quote comes from Proverbs 16:18. The King James version of this Biblical scripture warns that "Pride goeth before destruction, and a haughty spirit before a fall." This is a classic theme of Greek tragedies, people in the Bible, and today.

Many people are overly confident of their own righteousness and look down on others. Jesus told this parable:

Two men went up to the temple to pray, one a Pharisee and the other a tax collector. The Pharisee stood by himself and prayed: 'God, I thank you that I am not like other people—robbers, evildoers, adulterers—or even like this tax collector. I fast twice a week and give a tenth of all I get.'

But the tax collector stood at a distance. He would not even look up to heaven, but beat his breast and said, 'God, have mercy on me, a sinner.' Jesus said, "I tell you that this man, rather than the other, went home justified before God. For all those who exalt themselves will be humbled, and those who humble themselves will be exalted. (Luke 18:10-14)

The Pharisee's life was dominated by his ego. His prayer was all about himself. He had an air of superiority over others and he reminded God how pious he was. The tax collector knew he fell short, owned the times when he missed the mark, and asked God for help. Jesus showed the paradoxical nature of some spiritual truths when he said the humble will be exalted.

When one is run by one's ego, conceit is developed and one takes full possession of accomplishments. This creates a never-ending search for happiness because these experiences of fame and notoriety are fleeting. The ego continues to search for more earthly pleasures, which can end with a drunken stupor or drug bust plastered on magazine covers, or a sex scandal that ends marriages and careers. Trappist monk, Thomas Merton said, "Pride makes us artificial and humility makes us real."

Human strengths are needed to be able to live in the world. If these strengths are not attributed to the Divine, the ego will make you become of the world. This will create a person who is self absorbed and oblivious to the needs of others. Benjamin Franklin said, "A man wrapped up in himself makes a very small bundle."

Creating a divine union of one's human strengths with one's Divine Self, one will be able to live in the world in a more effortless manner, and will not be of the world because the Divine will be directing one's path.

English writer G.K. Chesterton wrote, "It is always the secure who are humble." The secure are people who have healthy strengths and practice spiritual disciplines to allow the Spirit to drive them This will bring the right people together at the right time to accomplish the right things.

Our culture engenders conformity. People find comfort in the norm. It is the well worn path. We are not meant to be the mean, median, or mode of anything. We are designed to create a union between our human nature and divine nature. We are designed to take care of our self while we are taking care of others. We are designed to be compassionate and love our neighbor. We are designed with our unique personality and talents that need to be expressed for the good of all. We are designed to develop human strengths and then tether them to our Divine Self which will get us out of our own way and then let the Divine lead us.

Barry Switzer, former football coach of the Oklahoma Sooners said, "Some people are born on third base and go through life thinking they hit a triple." This humorous and egocentric paradigm is all too common. The ego will likely thrive if one is born into a family of wealth and a high position in society. External rewards like recognition and status prop up the ego. By definition, this is the antithesis of a spiritual journey. This person might go to church, but he is probably not led by God because he is stuck in a label of Christian/Jew/ Muslim. He is stuck in worldly matters and too prideful and fearful to let go and follow "Thy will."

You have to "break down" to "break through" to a union with God. You have to admit your shortcomings, your egocentric strivings, and the pain you have experienced in life. Only by being humble will you forgive yourself and others. Only by being humble, owning when you have missed the mark, will you be able to depower your ego and tether your human strengths to your Divine Self. The true litmus test of whether or not you are operating from the Divine Self is being humble.

"Wash out your ego once in a while, as cleanliness is next to godliness not just in body but in humility as well," wrote Terri Guillemets. Freedom is bringing your ego to the light, giving it a good washing and letting go of it. Rinsing off the labels, titles, old grudges, conceit, judgments, and your favorite of the seven deadly sins. (We all have a favorite one. Do you know which one is yours?) You might want to pre-soak a part of the ego which is hardest to loosen and let go of. Hang out the ego to dry and shine some light on it because as Supreme Court Justice Louis Brandeis said, "Sunlight is the best disinfectant." The reason all of this is important is because humility creates the closest possible intimacy with your Divine Self and God.

The divine union of our human nature and our spiritual nature will lead us to the road of freedom where we can walk humbly and be open to forgive, serve others, and live the prayer, "Thy will be done."

Action Plan

1. Draw a larger circle of acceptance around a situation or person that you are resisting.
2. Make a list of your values. Pick one and fully live it today.
3. Admit to where you have missed the mark. Be humble and ask for God's help to forgive yourself and give you the strength to make better decisions

CHAPTER TEN

The cause of all suffering

Siddhartha Gautama was born in India around 560 B.C. As a young adult when he saw old age, death, and disease, he vowed to study human nature for the purpose of alleviating suffering. He first studied underneath the greatest Yoga teachers. He reached the deepest levels of meditation and altered consciousness. He was not satisfied because he realized this provided only a temporary escape. These strategies and techniques were not a permanent cure for human suffering. He became an ascetic and vowed to give up the needs of the body. He was down to eating only one grain of rice per day which almost killed him. Later, he accepted food, sat down under a bodhi tree and promised to meditate until the answer to suffering came to him.

After seven days, he reached a profound awareness of the nature of our human reality and the solution to the problem of suffering came to him. He then became known as Buddha, which means the Awakened One. He spent the remaining forty-five years of his life teaching and helping others.

The Buddha's solution to suffering is within the Four Noble Truths. The first Noble Truth states that life is suffering. There is a universal dissatisfaction that permeates the human existence. Our perception of change, other's actions, illness, old age, death, and pain creates suffering. Not getting what we want and getting what we don't want create suffering.

The second Noble Truth states that attachment is the cause of all suffering. Buddha realized that we get mentally and emotionally attached to many, many things. A good way to describe this truth is to pretend you have your favorite coffee cup in front of you. Further pretend that you love that coffee cup because your spouse gave it to you, it has your favorite picture or quote on it, and you have many, many fond memories with it. In your belief system, you can't accept if anything negative would happen to this cup. You are so attached to it that if anything happened to it, you would suffer. It is as if you have grabbed on to the coffee mug with your hands and are literally attached to it. If you're attached to it, and it doesn't turn out the way you want it to, it metaphorically breaks and turns into sharp shards, what does it do to your hands? It bloodies them. You suffer.

We are now going to practice changing the scenario. Keep that coffee cup in front of you, but let go of it by two or three inches. Keep your hands around the coffee cup, because you are highly interested in it. If it starts to fall off your desk or end table, you want to be near enough to be able to catch it. If you are non-attached, not in a laissez-faire, I-don't-care way (move your hands as far away from the cup as you can), but in an I-care-about-this-coffee-cup-but-I'm-not-going-to-be-attached way, now if the coffee mug metaphorically breaks and become shards what will it do to your hands? You will still feel the experience because we are sentient beings, but you will not suffer. A Buddhist precept wisely explains this; "Pain is inevitable, suffering is optional."

We mentally and emotionally attach to many things every day. For example, if you are driving down a street at 40 miles per hour, happy as a lark, highly interested in the driving experience (your hands are two to three inches from that metaphorical cup), and another person pulls out in front of you and drives 25 miles per hour, what do you typically do? Your thoughts become attached to the other person's slow driving. You grab the "cup" and get mad, honk your horn, tailgate him, or a variety of other things. You are suffering. If you practice the Third Noble Truth, which is to practice non-attachment, let go of the "cup," you will get your serenity back, and become a safer driver.

Another example is bed time for your children. They are watching television downstairs and you tell them nicely at the top of the stairs,

"Kids, its 9:00, time to come up and get ready for bed." They yell back, "Be right up." Five minutes pass and you don't see them. You state again, "C'mon kids, it's time to get ready for bed. Turn off the TV and come upstairs." They yell, "Ok, we'll be right up." Another five minutes pass and you "grab the cup" because they have not come upstairs. You judge (Chapter Four) their behavior as wrong, which makes your thoughts become attached to them not obeying. You are now angry, stomp downstairs, and yell at your kids. In this example, if you would have remained highly interested in your children's behaviors, cared deeply about their welfare and bedtime, and remained two to three inches from that "cup." Your discerning thoughts might have come up with, "Kids, if you don't come up now, you will lose TV for a week." Most probably, the children would have scampered upstairs, and your home would have remained peaceful.

There are two types of attachment. The first aspect is craving, our desiring for things to be other than what they are. For example, in the previous example, you are attached to your children's non-compliance and you have grabbed onto the "cup" and trying to pull them to you. The other aspect is aversion, or hatred. For example, the slow car in front of you creates anger and you have grabbed onto the "cup" and tried to push it away.

In both examples of attachment; craving and aversion, Buddha said if you want to achieve freedom and not suffer, let go of your attachment to how you think the world should work and the self-defeating attachment to outcomes. Be highly interested in life, but do not be attached. Communicate your ideas, work for what you think is right, but do so in a non-attached manner. You will have way less baggage to carry around on your journey.

Athletes know this truth. When a golfer or a tennis player is attached to her performance and says to herself, "I have to make this putt," or "I have to get this second serve in," she will tend to tense her muscles, grab the racket or putter too strongly, and her mind will be full of "I have to..." thoughts. Paradoxically, she is much more likely to miss the putt or double fault while she is attached to her thoughts and an outcome.

When she is highly interested in making the putt, but not attached to a certain outcome, she will more probably have relaxed muscles, a clear mind, and swing the putter in a better manner.

Effortless effort occurs in sports, work, art, parenting or other activities when a person is involved in a non-attached manner. It takes effort to play a good game of tennis. It takes effort to solve problems at work. It takes effort to raise self-reliant children. And, when the bumps on the road occur, create a space of awareness (Chapter Six); become deeply interested, open, unafraid, and then you will experience them in a non-personal manner. You will then more effectively use your human strengths of communication skills, conflict resolution, and boundary setting. Staying non-attached will create a clear, empty mind (Chapter Five) so you can stay connected to your Divine Self and prayerfully receive help from God.

The ego does not operate this way. The person living in this ego state is fearful and does not want to give up control. He takes everything personally. For example, the driver that merged into the lane you were in and drove 25 miles per hour. The ego thinks, "That old man pulled in *my* lane." "How dare he slow *me* down. He is going to make *me* late."

Your humanity that is in union with your Divine Self will practice being non-attached to the slow driver. You will not take the situation personally. You will practice your discernment skills, slow down, or change lanes. This is freedom.

The parent whose ego is dominant will perceive the children's non-compliant behavior as personal "*My* kids are not obeying *me*." "I'm mad because now I'll have less of *my* own time tonight."

The human strengths that are tethered to your Divine Self will be non-attached, yet highly interested in the situation. You will not perceive the children as personally trying to provoke you. You will use parental power wisely and creatively find a consequence if they choose to further not obey.

Whatever is, is. And can be made better. Practicing non-attachment is accepting what is. And, the practice includes staying close enough mentally and emotionally to "what is"—the metaphorical cup—to be involved, and try to help the situation.

For example, there are many social injustices. There are lower socio-economic children whose families cannot afford to buy them bicycles.

What is, is. And can be made better. One could be highly interested in this and start a program that collects used bikes, fix them up, and donate them to needy children. This is an example of a union between the Divine Self and human strengths.

There is graffiti on buildings in a section of town. One could be attached to the eye sores, judge the situation, and berate the "delinquents" who de-faced the property. Or one could see the graffiti in a non-attached manner, be highly interested in beautifying the neighborhood or stopping the negative behavior, and try to make the situation better by getting a church or civic group to re-paint the vandalized areas. This is another example of the divine union.

Edwin Friedman, an ordained Jewish Rabbi, wrote in *Generation to Generation* how the concept of systematic family therapy applies to the emotional life of a church's congregation. The family systems approach states that each person in a family must differentiate from the others. Each person must define his or her own goals and values. Each person must know his or her own personal strengths and manifest them in the world. Then each person must maintain a non-anxious presence in anxiety producing situations. This means each family member must stay non-attached when other family members are acting out or showing their own quirky personality traits. Finally, each person must take maximum responsibility for one's own destiny and emotional well being. This means he or she stays close enough to communicate, set boundaries, and make "I" statements so others know what is needed, and compromise when it is appropriate.

When we become attached to life situations, we are then like the monkey in the jungle who is so easily hunted by simply chaining a banana stalk to a tree. The monkey grabs the banana stalk fiercely, trying to wrestle it away, screaming as he hears the hunters approach, bellowing as he is slain. The monkey never realizes—we never realize—that to simply let go might lead to freedom and safety.

The ego lives in the past and the future. If someone has hurt us in the past, the ego will be attached, hold on to the old wound and maintain the identity of victim. The spiritual practices of letting go, being non-attached, forgiving, and turning the other cheek, are foreign concepts to the ego. Ann Landers wrote, "Hanging onto resentment is letting someone you despise live rent-free in your head."

There are toxic people in the world who are hurtful, pernicious, and even destructive. With these people it is important to be more non-attached than with others. Instead of holding your hands two to three inches from the metaphorical coffee cup, your hands should be five or six inches away. These toxic "coffee cups" have a tendency to have bigger explosions—bigger and sharper shards—which means one has to be more emotionally detached. For example, if a person in your extended family is toxic—but not too toxic—you may still show respect and show up for Thanksgiving dinner. But instead of staying three or four hours, you might stay for an hour or two and have an exit strategy already planned. Don't be attached to their negative attitudes or behaviors. Be non-attached and stay for a shorter period of time before they have a tendency to act out their problems.

The fourth Noble Truth contains the answer to how we stay non-attached and live a life of freedom. It is known as the Eightfold Path. It consists of Right Understanding and Right Thinking which are related to wisdom. The next three, Right Speech, Right Action and Right Livelihood, speak to moral conduct. The final three, Right Effort, Right Mindfulness, and Right Concentration, are mental disciplines.

Being mentally and emotionally attached is the opposite of being free. Freedom comes when a family member says something inappropriate, and you don't get disturbed. Freedom comes if it rains when you wanted to go camping and you smoothly create another fun weekend. Freedom comes when your boss is being stern and you don't take it personally. Freedom comes when you forgive yourself and others.

Let go and experience freedom. Enjoy the moments of peace and serenity. You are human and you will soon get attached again. Smile, and let go of the "coffee cup." With practice, you will more often be lovingly non-attached. You will be happier because of your divine union. This is the road to freedom.

Action Plan

1. Place a real coffee mug in front of you. Name what attachment it represents to you. Grab the mug and experience what that feels like. Now let go of the mug and experience how that feels.

2. During your next conflict with a family member, communicate and try to resolve the issue in a highly interested, yet nonattached manner.

3. Whatever is, is. And can be made better. Practice accepting something in your life <u>and</u> making it better.

CHAPTER ELEVEN

Practicing non-attachment

It's easy to be connected to God and be non-attached to ego's desires and aversions while you are in hiking a beautiful trail on a sunny spring day. It's easy to go with the flow after a long day of work and all you're doing is watching television.

It is much more difficult to be one with God while your spouse is asking more of you, your children are disobeying, your checkbook is in the red, your boss is being bossy, and the driver ahead of you is, in your very wise opinion, driving too slow.

In this chapter, I will present some typical situations to show how ego attachment occurs which will create suffering. The strategies are shared to let go of the "coffee mug" which will allow the divine union to occur and reduce suffering in your life.

Marriage

Marriage is the ultimate relationship where the human strengths of communication, conflict resolution, compromise, and budget management, to name a few, are needed to a very high degree. It takes two committed partners working together for the marriage to evolve, deal with issues, and not just survive, but thrive. By definition, the ego thinks only about self. Within a marriage, this is the recipe for disaster because a marriage is not about self, it is about a union of two people. Our Divine Self will naturally think of taking care of both the self and others. The question for every marriage is, will the necessary and needed human strengths of each spouse be driven by the ego or the Divine Self?

With the lengthy list of responsibilities around the house, the ego will keep a scorecard of who has done the most work. For example, a wife could think, "This weekend, I drove the kids to two events, cooked five meals, and vacuumed the house. My husband only mowed the lawn. I am up 8 to 1." This uneven scorecard could make the wife feel angry. She might become aggressive and lash out at him. "I cooked for *you*. I cleaned up after *you*," she might yell. She might become passive aggressive and withhold intimacy. The husband will be clueless as to why he is being treated this way.

The ego's orientation is only about self. The Divine Self is wiser and knows the ego insidiously structures life with divisions of self and others. The Divine Self doesn't separate but utilizes a strategy of doing things for the marriage. This will automatically create a detachment from the ego because it includes a strategy of union. Judgments (Chapter Four) will more likely fall by the wayside because scorekeeping is no longer used. The Divine Self has the gift of discernment and if the work load becomes too lopsided, healthy communication will ensue with both parties taking ownership.

"DO THINGS FOR THE MARRIAGE."

Any fears of a failed marriage, lack of love, or a destiny of indentured servitude, will evaporate because the ego will no longer be in charge. The Divine Self united with our human strengths naturally creates a bond of love and with new awareness, the husband will use the strategy of "do things for the marriage" and the wedge that was dividing the marriage will get smaller.

The practice of forgiveness (6th of the Seven Core Beliefs) will more likely occur over the uneven work load because the other partner will have started to kick it in "for the marriage."

Communication will occur about what is happening in the present moment (4th of the Seven Core Beliefs) because all old scorecards will have been thrown away and there are no new scorecards that can be pulled out to be used in the future.

For example, the husband proactively creates a conversation with his wife. "Hon, you've been talking for weeks about painting our living room. You know that is the last thing I would like to do. But, it's important to you—I want to do it for our marriage—so let's get it done this weekend". Or, the wife knows her husband gave up his poker night once the children were born. She might say, "You haven't had a boys' night in a long time. I can take the kids over to my parents' house for the evening if you want to have a poker night at our house." In each case, the other spouse will feel honored and want to keep creating kind acts for the other.

Money

Within life partnerships, communication is the over-arching and biggest on-going dynamic that can cause problems. The next two biggest issues are sex and money. In ego-driven households, money beats out sex as the number one issue.

The ego does not have substance so it tries to attach to other things. Money is a typical place where the ego attaches because our culture puts so much emphasis and power on money. The more perceived power, the more the ego wants to attach.

Because of this ego attachment, a person can end up measuring his self worth by his net worth. To raise one's net worth, one must work long hours and do (Chapter Two) many, many work related projects.

The ego can never acquire enough money to be satisfied. As a result, someone who is attached to money can easily come to see the whole world in terms of scarcity. The ego sees even the spiritual gifts of love, patience, forgiveness, kindness, and generosity as scare.

The Divine Self knows the importance of money. The Divine Self knows money must be respected because one must live *in* the world. And, the Divine Self does not worship money, so one is not at-risk for becoming *of* the world. The ego's unconscious craving and love of money is abandoned. Living in a divine union, good and functional decision making will occur, and the stress of money will no longer be the number one conflict within the marriage.

The best and most functional strategy I have found is to perceive money as numbers. This will create detachment from the ego and reduce emotions that we attach to money. The couple will sit at the kitchen table, study their checkbook, and will make sure they have more income *numbers* than expense *numbers* every month. When they do, they wisely might save some numbers for a rainy day. A couple could ask themselves, "Do we have enough numbers to purchase a new washing machine?" If so, a decision might be made to spend those extra numbers and purchase that item. If a couple doesn't have enough numbers, the washing machine is not purchased. The emotions (Chapter Four) are taken out of the situation.

Viewing money as numbers neutralizes the situation. For example, number 20 is not good or bad. It is just the number 20. Number 100 is more than 20, but it is still neutral. If something costs $100.00, a person doesn't overreact to the cost. He counts his numbers and decides if he has enough numbers to purchase the item. He might decide to not spend those numbers and save the numbers for something else down the road.

The Divine Self realizes the wisdom of balance and living the middle way between the extremes. The Divine Self does not wish for poverty (unless one has made a conscious pledge of poverty), nor does it ask for monetary riches. The middle way is abundance, where a person knows there will always be enough for what is needed.

The Divine Self lives by the paradox, in giving you receive. A person in divine union more easily contributes a larger portion of his income. By sharing his resources, it opens up the natural, cyclical flow of life. He will earn money, and share money. Earn money and share money.

<u>Work</u>

Elsewhere, I wrote about the paradox, "Choose a job you love, and you will never have to work another day."[1] The ego does not understand this truth. The ego has our mind thinking in terms of fear and scarcity. The ego cannot understand the both-and thinking of paradoxes and views work as a four letter word. The ego mind thinks in an either-or manner and looks at situations as win-lose instead of trying to listen, compromise, and create outcomes where everyone wins.

---

[1]   *Little Me Can Live a Big Life,* iUniverse, 2009, page 79

The ego creates either-or hierarchies and sub-groups. Boss-employee, company-customer, white collar-blue collar, and labor-administration are examples of this duality. This creates win-lose outcomes, and a self-fulfilling prophecy of work being hard and full of suffering.

The Divine Self knows every human is given gifts and abilities. The Divine Self wants to be in union with one's human nature and utilize those abilities in the world.

This viewpoint will detach the ego from the workplace and will create opportunities to manifest one's talents.

An employee who is connected to his Divine Self knows everyone is created differently and conflicts will occur. He knows the conflicts are not "good" or "bad", but there is a lesson within the conflict to help the organization. In comparison to the ego-driven person who detests conflicts, because he sees them as win-lose, and only wants to get his way. The person connected to his spiritual nature embraces conflicts and asks everyone to share their thoughts and perspective freely. By doing this, the group will create synergy which will be used as a springboard for better ideas, products, and a healthier workplace.

A person living in divine union's number one goal at work is not to make money. The goal is to do the work you love, do it well, and the money will then follow.

Children

Kahlil Gibran wrote, "Your children are not your children." This statement does not compute to the ego of a parent. Again, because the ego does not have substance, it needs to attach to something. Along with money, children are the prime target for such attachment.

The parents' egos perceive the success of their children as their successes, and failures as their own failures. Many fights, unnecessary emotional reactions, and estranged relationships are created because of this ego attachment. Another example of ego's ownership is when parents project their earlier unmet needs onto their children. They do this when they see their children as extensions of them. When this dynamic occurs, the boy will then be responsible to be the accomplished football player that the dad never achieved. Mom might project the necessity to make straight A's because of her missed opportunity to study at an esteemed university. And so on, and so on.

The Divine Self knows that children are gifts from God. They are important gifts that need to be loved, nurtured, disciplined, and allowed to find their own talents and abilities.

Parents who are in divine union, know how quickly the approximately twenty years of child rearing responsibilities go and they practice treasuring each and every day. They are open to differences in their children and try to help grow the different strengths and abilities. They know the three most important ways to raise their children are: 1) by example, 2) by example, and 3) by example.

Acknowledging that our children came through us, but they are not us, is a good way to create detachment from the ego. Acknowledging that we are responsible for our children, but they are not ours, will keep our egos at bay.

A parent in divine union does not take "no" from a two year old personally. The parent of an adolescent prays for her teenager all the time, but even more so on a Saturday night. If the teen makes a bad decision there isn't a button in the parent to be pushed (an ego to be twanged), and the parent doesn't react from an unstable emotional place. The parent helps her child, gives appropriate consequences, provides more education if needed, and continues to love her child.

Children want to be on the road to freedom from their parents. We need to see the divinity within them, and continuously reflect it to them. If we do, maybe their egos won't be as strong, insidious, and malevolent as ours.

We also need to help our children develop their human strengths so when we push them out of the nest, they will successfully fly.

Driving

Driving is a much smaller, and one could say less important, dynamic in our life. But the road is a great laboratory to see how the ego works. Every day, I use my driving time as a barometer on how strong or weak my ego is working.

Driving a car is a ripe place for the ego to reign because of the perceived separateness between the cars and the other drivers. With the ego in charge, judgments can run rampant within a fifteen minute drive; "Move faster, grandma!" "That asshole cut me off." "I can't believe

I've hit every red light in the city." These ego driven thoughts create lots of baggage: anger, hostility, and a drive that is full of negativity.

The Divine Self understands the connectedness to all other drivers. The Divine Self united with the human strengths of driving creates an awareness that others are doing the best they can. Forgiveness (6th Core Belief) follows because you become aware that you have cut someone off in the past, or you drove slowly when you were lost.

Detachment from the ego will more naturally occur and stressful reactions will be less likely to happen because you are peaceful and realize every road you literally drive on is a metaphorical road to freedom.

Action Plan

1. Practice doing things for the marriage.
2. Practice seeing money as numbers and make better decisions within how many numbers you have.
3. As your child more often what he wants to do instead of directing his life so much.

CHAPTER TWELVE

Paradox: Embracing Both-And Thinking

The Relative and the Absolute Realms

A paradox is a statement that is seemingly contradictory and yet is perhaps true. A paradox embraces "both-and" thinking instead of "either-or" thinking. For example, I am paradoxically both generous and selfish. I am both strong and weak. I am both a saint and a sinner. Paradoxes are two ends of the same continuum. They are interdependent and co-exist with one another. Each depends upon the other for meaning (you cannot understand night without day).

Either-or thinking is dualistic in nature. This thinking process separates, divides, and puts people and experiences into boxes. For example, in an election year, a state is labeled either blue or red. We know all states are various shades of purple. We tend to judge things as pleasurable or painful. But, for example, an exercise program is initially painful and then we experience the pleasure of a more fit body.

The Taoists in ancient China created a theory based on the construct of two polar complements, called Yin and Yang. These opposites exist in relation to each other. All things are seen as parts of the whole. No entity can be isolated from its relationship to its opposite. *Both* the yin *and* the yang—the entire circle—are embraced. The polarity has been harnessed which creates synergy. This interaction produces a total effect greater than the sum of its parts.

An important aspect of life vital to ones understanding of how to live a life of freedom is a Buddhist belief that states there are paradoxically two realms of existence: a relative, conventional realm, and an absolute, ultimate realm.

The relative realm is dualistic in nature. For example, one's spiritual nature and human nature are separate. There is a division between good and bad, desirable and undesirable, painful and pleasurable. A paradigm of this realm is to perceive others as separate, and to draw boundaries between nations and religions. (The United States is different from Canada and Mexico).

The absolute realm is paradoxical in nature. There is a union between the human and the divine. The two ends of the continuum of good/bad, dark/light, pass/fail, saint/sinner, are embraced and held in unity. (We all live on the same planet).

There is a wonderful story that illuminates these two realms. This story is told in different ways in *Sadhana: A Way to God,* by Anthony de Mello, *Way of the Peaceful Warrior,* by Dan Millman, and the movie, *Charlie Wilson's War.* Here is an amalgamation of these three sources that show the relative and absolute realms.

There is an ancient Chinese story of an old farmer who only had one horse and one son to help him on his farm. One day the horse escaped and all the farmer's neighbors felt sad for him. They told him they were sorry for his bad luck. The wise farmer said, "Good luck? Bad luck? Who knows? We shall see." A couple of days later, the horse came back with five wild mares. This time the neighbors congratulated the farmer on his good luck. His wise reply was, "Good luck? Bad luck? Who knows? We shall see." A week later, his son was taming one of the wild horses and got bucked off and broke his leg. Again the neighbors expressed their sadness and thought this was very bad luck. The farmer responded the same way, "Good luck? Bad luck? Who knows? We shall see." Some weeks later, the army came through his small village and rounded up all the young men to go off to war. When they found the farmer's son with a broken leg, they left him behind. At the relative realm, we judge experiences as "good luck" or "bad luck." At the ultimate realm, we do not know. We shall see.

This story shows how the ego is a critic. In the relative realm, things are always changing. The ego creates bi-polar like reactions to life. The ego instantly will judge it was "bad" the horse ran away. Then the ego will judge the five wild mares as "good." Then "bad" again, and then "good." This way is exhausting and maddening, and one needlessly suffers.

The ego exists in the relative realm. The ego makes judgments of "good" and "bad" at every life circumstance. Yet there is a Greater Intelligence that doesn't see life in such a limited and dichotomized manner. We've all heard stories about a person who left late for work, only to miss a huge accident on the highway. Or a person who missed a job interview, only to find a better job later. Or a person who chipped a tooth, which led him to meet someone in the dentist's office he later marries. Good? Bad? We shall see.

Everything is ephemeral, transitory, and ever changing in the relative realm. For example, we grow old, friends move, and our children become adults. Existence in the absolute realm is unchanging, enduring, and abiding. For example, love lasts and continues through time and space, and God is ever present. By definition, the relative realm does not include the absolute realm, but the absolute realm includes the relative realm in its non-dualistic existence. Our goal is to hold the two realms together during our experiences in life. (I live in a certain part of the earth—the United States—*and* I am a citizen of the world.)

When I spend time with an adolescent in a counseling session, I will say "I'm sorry" when the teen shares something tragic that has occurred in his life. Many times the teen will reply, "It's all good." Unbeknownst to the teen, he responded from the absolute realm. In the relative realm, it is sad that his dog died, or an older brother went overseas to fight in a war, or his dad was laid off from his job.

We need to acknowledge the relative realm and use appropriate coping skills, express feelings, or communicate to resolve conflicts. Simultaneously, we need to embrace the absolute realm and trust in God and lean into His/Her understanding. We need to live *in* the world: hold a job, pay the bills, change the oil in the car. Buddhists call this "chop wood, carry water." But we are not to be *of* the world. We need to free ourselves from the illusions of "I," duality, and other tricks the ego plays on us. We need to awaken to the absolute realm and then competently and compassionately live in the relative realm.

> # WE NEED TO AWAKEN TO THE ABSOLUTE REALM AND THEN COMPETENTLY AND COMPASSIONATELY LIVE IN THE RELATIVE REALM.

Your physical body resides in the relative realm. One of the important reasons it's important to take care of the body by exercising and eating right, is so you don't get sick or hurt and stay stuck in the relative realm. It is much more difficult to do our spiritual practices while we have a headache or stomachache.

In Chapter Three, we emphasized that our sense of "I"—which is our ego—is a subjective identity. One experiences a never-ending succession of transitory "I's." The ego is always changing, impermanent, and partial. Ego experiences are nonenduring; one needs to have an identity separate from others. This is how one lives in the relative realm. The Divine Self—our being—is timeless and eternal. The Divine Self knows everything is interconnected: God, nature, self, and others. St. Francis of Assisi said, "In giving you receive." This paradox is absolute truth because everything is one—there are no separate things. This is how one lives in the absolute realm.

The union of the human and the divine, and the union of the relative and absolute realms, is clearly our task in life. It takes the spaciousness of God to be able to hold the good and the bad, the dark and the light, the sacred and the profane, the relative and the absolute. The divine within you—the Divine Self—can hold the two ends of the continuum. When the Divine Self holds the opposites inside of you, then you can help and hold them for others.

Spiritual practices are the avenue by which to access the absolute realm while living in the relative realm. Meditation, being grateful, and forgiving yourself and others are important disciplines. Meditation allows you to watch with detached interest what occurs in your life. While you are detached, the relative realm is not as sticky and judgments are less likely to occur. The practice of being grateful connects you back to the Divine, and with that union it is easier to accept what happens in our life and not get attached to the negative. Forgiveness allows you to heal from the pains of the relative realm, merge into the absolute realm, and trust in God's plan for your life.

Zentatsu Richard Baker, an American Soto Zen Roshi said, "Enlightenment is an accident. Meditation makes you accident prone." You will be more "accident prone" to create the union of the relative and absolute realms by practicing many spiritual disciplines over a period of time.

Freedom, which is our true nature, is realized by remaining aware of the absolute realm while working and playing in the relative realm. Glen Frey sings in The Eagles' song, *Already Gone*, "So often times it happens that we live our lives in chains, And we never even know we have the key." You now have the key. Practice. Continue to practice. And continue some more. Before you know it, you will have less baggage, you will have shed all the old "concrete and dirt." You will be one with your Divine Self. This is the road to freedom.

Action Plan

1. Take time to understand these two realms and practice being able to live in both.
2. Be grateful and give thanks in all circumstances. Every day for an entire week, make a list of ten things in which you are grateful.
3. Next time you find yourself chained, quite blaming something external and spend some time finding the key you already have.

CHAPTER THIRTEEN

Homo Sapiens

We are homo sapiens. Homo is a Latin word that means "man" or "human." Sapiens is a Latin word that means "wise species." We call ourselves a wise species. Where is the proof of this declaration?

For thousands of years, we, this "wise species" has been killing each other because of a desire for more land, or a belief that others were worshiping the wrong God, or simply because one homo sapiens pissed off another homo sapiens.

For thousands of years, we, this "wise species" has made a certain skin color more valuable than another, or created a caste system based on the family into which you were born, or more recently decided to disregard the environment based on economic gain.

Because we have edged God out, we have lost our wisdom. We have empowered our ego to a point that we are at risk for destroying our species. How have we lost our connection to the Divine and become so mired in our humanness?

Plato wrote The Cave, which is a wonderful allegory found in his best known work, *The Republic*. Plato tells a story about how we are all prisoners in a cave. We are bound and shackled and stand facing a wall of the cave so that we can see only what is directly in front of us on that wall. Behind us is a raised walkway upon which puppets move—not only wooden figures but also figures of houses, trees, work places, sports arenas, and all the other things in the world.

Behind these figures is a blazing fire that casts its light onto the figures, projecting their shadows onto the wall. It is these shadows that we see and it is these shadows that we think are real. The shadows are as close as the prisoners get to viewing reality. What they take to be real is in fact an illusion.

Plato asks us to imagine that someone frees us from our shackles and turns us around so that we now face the fire. At first our eyes would be overwhelmed by the light and we would have difficulty fully seeing the puppets. But as our eyes grew accustomed to the light, we would begin to see the different puppets, the fire, and then know the shadows for what they truly are.

What if a wise person were to lead us on a journey out of the cave? The journey would be difficult initially, with much stumbling. And if we succeeded and came out into the sunlight, we would once again be blinded. Our eyes would be so overcome with light, that only in time could we look directly at things—reality—themselves.

If we should come so far, Plato says we would want to remain in the sunlight and never re-enter the darkness of the cave. We would choose to go back only in the hope of leading others out.

But if we return to the prisoners and begin to tell them what we have seen, they would not understand us, for how can one tell people that the only thing they know—the shadows—are not real? We cannot put sight into blind eyes, or knowledge into people's heads. We can only turn the prisoners around so that they will look in a different direction.

Our ego has deluded us and has us believing in the shadows of "I" experiences (Chapter Three), judging things as right or wrong (Chapter Four), being busy and full of oneself (Chapter Five), that we can control life (Chapter Eleven), separate from others and God, fears, living in the past or the future.

If you live in the United States or in another industrialized country, you are most probably living in a "cave" where the fire casts huge shadows depicting the importance of Gross National Product (GNP). Many shadows are thrown up on the wall showing people working long hours, buying many products, bigger houses, and shinier cars, all to create a story of success. This story line allows one to have limited time with his family, experience stress related health problems, and go long periods without laughing. When led out of the cave and into the light, the folly of this story is soon realized.

You ask your wise leader if there is a better story in which to live. She leads you to the country of Bhutan, which is located in southern Asia by the Himalayas. In 1972, Bhutan's former king developed Gross National Happiness (GNH) to create an indicator that measures quality of life for his people. He was committed to building an economy that was true to his culture based on Buddhist spiritual values. The primary goal was to create a society where material and spiritual development occur together to complement and reinforce each other.

This is an example of exiting a cave and adjusting to the light. The decision to create an economy where the material and the spiritual are united is a prime example that we are capable of being a "wise species." I encourage you to move to a better place and leave the cave where the ego is the puppeteer and projects stories of lies and illusions.

Jihad is an Islamic term that has many meanings. The mystical Sufi sect of Islam adopted the interpretation that has an internal meaning. Muhammad said jihad describes the warrior who is at war with himself. He uses a sword to slay the ego. I invite everyone to create a holy war with themselves in which to disarm the ego and claim their Divine Self.

When we read our history books, we can see countless examples of human foolishness, recklessness, and madness. The only way we can learn from history and be able to truly live as a "wise species" is to claim the transcendent within us and grow that light. Live in the light. Walk in the light. *Be* the light (Chapter Two). Then, and only then, will our ego be de-powered and with God's grace, we will create the divine union between our human nature and our spiritual nature. We will not only survive, but we will thrive as a species.

When we create a divine union, we will feel the exhilaration of its potential. We will experience the freedom of not being in bondage to our ego. We will want to share our exciting truth with others. But often our message will fall on deaf ears because most people live the well trodden path of an ego existence. We might soon find we are living our life with one foot in the ego world, and one foot in the spiritual world.

We all want to feel accepted by others, and to experience the comfort of our old habitual patterns of living. The promise of the divine union pulls us forward while the old habits pull us back.

A truth from a pun will help us with this dilemma. A baseball player was playing catch and wondered why the baseball was getting bigger and bigger, until it hit him. The moral of this pun is whatever we look at will get bigger and bigger—until we get hit by it! If we look toward spiritual development and creating a divine union with our human strengths, this way of being in the world will get bigger. When a thought comes into our mind about the material world, we need to gently let it go, and remember this pun. We then need to move into our spiritual practices of praying, focusing on our breathing, loving the person in front of us, and other practices that assist us on this new path.

When do you experience the holy? When you are with a small child? In nature, or while exercising? In church, or at the non-profit agency where you volunteer and help others? Paying something forward? Notice that you are outside of yourself—your ego—in all of these examples. Focus on these activities and sooner than later, your feet will not be in two different worlds, but planted firmly in the divine union between your human nature and your spiritual nature.

Buddhists, Hindus, and people of other eastern faiths prayerfully put their opened left and right palms together by their hearts and bow when they greet someone and when they depart. They say "Namaste," which means, "The God in me meets the God in you. The Spirit in me meets the same Spirit in you."

This human interaction weaves together the divinity that is within each and every one of us. One could say one of the hands represents our human nature uniting with the other hand which represents our divine nature. Millions of human beings who live in the eastern part of the world realize this truth while millions in the industrialized west have forgotten this truth because they have been living in caves.

People of ancient Greece separated the divine from the human by placing the gods on Mount Olympus. Prometheus is the protagonist of one of the early mythological tales. He was known as the champion of mankind because he stole fire from Zeus and gave it to man. Aeschylus wrote in the Greek tragedy *Prometheus Bound* that he also taught humans the arts of civilization: writing, science, agriculture, mathematics, and medicine.

Prometheus was so clever and wily that the modern word Promethean means creative, boldly original, imaginative, and life enhancing. Let us all exert Promethean efforts to bring the gods off Mount Olympus, not project our divinity outside of our self and onto our minister/priest/rabbi and the pulpit where he or she stands, and re-claim the Divine which resides within us.

Let us create a divine union. This is how we will be able to live in the world and not be of the world. This is the road to freedom.

Namaste.

Action Plan

1. Name some "shadows" in your life that you think are created by the large fire of culture.
2. Be aware when your ego starts to take over. For example, you are in a meeting and you are judging yourself on how you compare with others. Use the jihad sword and disarm the ego and move to loving yourself and others.
3. Practice interacting with people in the state of mind and heart of "The God in me meets the God in you."

OVERVIEW OF OUR HUMAN DEVELOPMENT

The development of one's personality is extremely complex. Research shows that experiences in the womb, genetics, early childhood experiences, traumatic events, culture, birth order, one's thinking process, and the interaction of all of these have impacts on personality development.

Philosophers and psychologists are intrigued as to how two siblings from the same gene pool and same environment can turn out to be so different. Is it because of a gene that skipped a generation and then showed up in the second born? Is it because mom and dad parented the first born differently? Is it because there were more children in the neighborhood for the first born to play with? Is it because the second born was sick during the first year of his life? Is it because culture rewarded the athletic abilities of the first born more than the music abilities of the second born? It is a complex interaction between all of these dynamics. People who live in eastern cultures like India and Tibet believe karma from past lives influence our current personality.

In the next seven chapters, various experiences that occur in people's lives will be looked at in the context of their human development. While reading these chapters, think about your life experiences. You will be asked where you think you land on the continuum of each strength. Strategies will be discussed to help heal, grow, rebuild, and evolve to a healthier state.

Our strengths are not in a constant state. Our strengths are fluid based upon the people and the environments we are in. For example, if we are interacting with a person we have faith in, our level of trust will increase. If we are conversing with a person with whom we do not have confidence, our trust level will not be as high. Take time to think about your strengths. Be open to your awareness of how each strength guides your life decisions. Spend a day or a week being highly aware of your level of trust and then, one at a time, every other strength. At the end of each chapter, a continuum is presented for you to draw an oval on the continuum that will represent your range of that specific human developmental strength in respect to how you think, feel, and act. Write the date above the opal/range. You might come back to this book and re-work the chapters and it will be helpful to see the personal growth that has occurred in your life.

As you read each chapter, pause and contemplate how you can make practical applications to your life. Take a risk and ask a friend for feedback. Get outside your box and take the initiative somewhere new in your life. Use each strength to create a union with your Divine Self.

Awareness of the level of one's strength may come from two sources. One source is self awareness. This is a person's ability to see one's life clearly and honestly. Insights as to why one acts or reacts in particular situations are more likely to come to a person who is self aware. These insights add to the level of self awareness, and hopefully motivate a person to grow and choose healthier and more functional behaviors. For example, if you squeeze an orange, the only thing that can come out is orange juice. Similarly, if someone "squeezes" you and anger comes out, the source of the anger is you. Even though objectively the other person is being a jerk, your angry response comes from you. Your angry response says everything about you and your wounded humanness. The other person is our teacher through whom we can learn our life lessons. (This statement does not include anger that comes from an injustice. Conscious and righteous anger directed at discrimination, bullying, unlawful behavior, or other injustices can be healthy and needed to right a wrong.)

Feedback from others is the second source of information. This is needed because all of us have difficulty seeing the forest from the trees in our own lives. We lose our clarity when someone pushes one of our buttons and we become angry. We automatically project our fear or resentment onto that person instead of looking inside ourselves for the source of those negative reactions.

Sometimes, insight into the root of the anger cannot be discerned and owned. Feedback from a trusted person who is more non-attached to the issue will help you put words to what got triggered within you and start the healing process.

A simple format to help us understand human behavior is Think-Feel-Act. Everything starts with a thought (7th of the Seven Core Beliefs). That thought creates a feeling(s). The thoughts and feelings lead us to act in a certain way. They are all interrelated. For example, the proverbial glass half-full or half-empty. One person might look at the glass with water and *think*, "The glass is half full." This could create a *feeling* of happiness, because there is enough water to quench his thirst. This will lead to the *action* of picking up the glass to drink the water. Another person might look at the glass with water and *think*, "The glass is half empty." This could create *feeling* of anger because there isn't enough water for him. This could lead to an *action* of yelling at a person, or walking away from the glass.

Feelings are messengers. If you are tired of feeling angry, distrustful, or sad, what are these feelings trying to tell you? Since everything starts with a thought, maybe you need to change how you think about certain unhealthy situations. If you're sad at work, do you need to change your thoughts about staying at that job? If you're mad at an individual, do you need to change your thoughts on how that other person should act? If you're disappointed with yourself, do you need to change your thoughts about yourself and take a calculated risk to get out of your rut?

Sometimes it's easier to act your way into a new way of thinking than to think yourself into a new way of acting. This is called "Fake it till you make it," or "act as if something is true." If you don't know if you can take the initiative and start a new project at work or at home, act as if you can. Start on the project and soon you might find that you think you can succeed. If you don't think you can start an exercise program, fake it—take a fifteen minute walk—until you think you can continue the exercise program.

At the end of each chapter, there are questions that will help you discern what you *think* about the position on the continuum of each human strength. There are questions about how you *feel* about the development of each human strength. And, there are questions to help you discern if you want to take any *actions* to create a better life. Since your thoughts, feelings, and actions are all interrelated, you may start with any of the questions. Find a question that resonates with you. Working on that question will affect the other two areas. Make sure you consciously remember there are two other areas that will change also. For example, if you select an *Act* question, down the road make sure you *think* about how the process is unfolding and how you *feel* about the results. This is a cross-training method that hopefully will bring you positive results.

If you change yourself, you will change your world. This journey is not for the faint-hearted. It is difficult to shine the light on ourselves. It is much easier to blame others and have the source of the problem lie outside of ourselves.

The reason many start this journey is because it is the road to freedom. This is the road where we are surrounded by love, forgiveness, and joy. This is the road where we will open ourselves up to something greater than ourselves. This is the road where we can let go of our baggage. We will more fully allow the Spirit to guide our steps. We will see more often the helpful clues the Universe is always communicating to us. We will be led to create win-win outcomes because we know we are all interconnected. We will trust our Higher Being and more fully live the prayer, "Thy will be done."

CHAPTER FOURTEEN

Erik Erikson: Expositor of Development of Human Strengths

Erik Erikson was born in 1902 near Frankfurt, Germany. He moved to Vienna as a young adult, and co-founded a progressive Montessori school which was created for the children of the rich patients who came to be analyzed by Sigmund and his daughter, Anna Freud.

The Freuds were impressed with Erikson. Anna asked him if he would be interested in beginning psychoanalysis with her and becoming a child analyst. This started Erik's career as an analyst, author, professor at Yale University Institute of Human Relations, Harvard and other universities, public speaker, and researcher of Sioux children in South Dakota.

As an educator, Erikson was interested in how young people might live healthier lives by strengthening and enriching their sense of self. In Erikson's theory, everyone is trying to understand and relate to themselves and others. The human strengths we develop give coherence and consistency to our life experiences, and have a unifying purpose that leads to the creation of our identity. He characterized these human strengths as a strong, vital, and positive force.

In Erikson's study of children, adolescents, and adults, he observed that there were certain critical times in development. Erikson concluded that throughout our lives, new environmental demands create crises that must be overcome. A specific virtue or human strength is developed during these periods. In the resolution of the conflicts, both positive and negative components are incorporated into the personality. What is vital and important is that a good ratio of positive to negative experiences is integrated into our personality.

Each of Erikson's eight stages of development is built on top of another. At each higher level, the human personality becomes more complex. If the human trait is not strengthened, it is likely to flounder and struggle, which will create problems in one's life. Each stage will be briefly described in this chapter and more fully defined and described in chapters two through chapter seven.

The first crisis of trust vs. mistrust occurs roughly during the first year of life. The human strength to be learned is trust: does one develop faith and confidence that one's needs will be met? Babies are totally dependent on their parents for care. If infants receive consistent, loving, and reliable care, trust is developed. If the care is inadequate or unreliable, a baby will perceive his world as hostile and unfriendly, and the child will develop a high degree of mistrust.

Even in loving and supportive homes, a parent cannot instantly be there for the child when he awakes scared, or when the wet diaper is uncomfortable, or when she bumps her head on the crib. This leads to a healthy dose of mistrust to be added to the trust that the child is developing. This is important because it would be unwise to have our children trust the world one hundred percent. There are snake-oil salesmen, bullies, and manipulative people who can harm others. An appropriate balance of trust and mistrust leads to the development of a healthy strength.

The second crisis of autonomy vs. shame and doubt occurs during the second and third years of life. This is when the child is learning to control his body to walk, talk, and use the toilet. The strength of autonomy is gained if the child is allowed to explore his surroundings with parental guidance. Labeling items to improve vocabulary, child proofing the home, putting away breakable items, and closely following the child on a walk outside are healthy ways to help build this strength.

Sometimes parents get mad when the child says "no," or become impatient if the child waddles away or even yell if the child soils his pants. The child will develop a high degree of shame and doubt if this occurs too often.

A time-out or stern words will create a healthy dose of shame and doubt which will help stop the child from gaining too much autonomy. We want our young children to learn to be interdependent with others, and to know to stay off a busy street…a fifty pound child will lose a fight with a two-ton car.

The third crisis of initiative vs. guilt occurs between ages three and five. Children are generating their own ideas and social roles. Preschoolers' activities are more goal oriented and their use of language becomes more sophisticated. If the child is rewarded for these behaviors, the strength of initiative is developed. If the child's environment is more impoverished, or the child receives negative feedback, the child will develop a higher degree of guilt.

A healthy dose of guilt needs to be integrated with the strength of initiative because there are cultural mores that need to be followed so one fits into society. And one needs to be interdependent and learn to work with others to help make a functional and healthy community.

The next stage of industry vs. inferiority happens during the elementary school years, between the ages of six and eleven. The important life skills of reading, writing, and arithmetic are taught during this stage. Important social skills are learned and children make more distinct comparisons between themselves and others. If the child learns these skills, the strength of industry is developed. If the child falls behind academically or socially, he or she will develop a sense of inferiority.

The best predictor of whether a person will earn a high school diploma is if he or she adequately learns to read during first grade. This strength and life skill of being industrious is highly important. It is easier to develop this if the previous strengths of trust, autonomy, and initiative have been developed.

The fifth crisis of identity vs. identity confusion is during adolescence. This is when our culture starts to ask the teens; "What major do you want to declare?" "What profession do you see yourself working towards?" "What school classes do you want to take?" If the teens starts to gain a sense of who they are, and what innate talents and gifts they have, it is easier for them to answer these questions of identity.

One's self-concept is learned by what is being mirrored to a person. If parents make negative comments to their child, he will probably take on a negative identity. If the parent-child relationship is weak and communication is limited, the child might be confused or ignorant about her identity. If the home environment is enriched and communication is honest and positive, the child will do a better job of knowing himself and what talents he has, which will lead to a choice of academic major and job profession.

The sixth crisis of intimacy vs. isolation occurs after adolescence and into the mid to late twenties. Typically, this stage is when a young adult is contemplating making a commitment with a life partner. If a person has a secure personal identity, she will more likely be open to risk love and intimacy with another. The strength of intimacy also includes the ability to create friendships and bonds with others.

If a person does not have the strength to gain intimate relationships, he will tend to become isolated. His interactions with others will be more superficial and he will become more self-absorbed. His relationship with his Higher Being will also be shallow or non-existent.

The seventh stage of generativity vs. stagnation is during the working years. The middle adult years includes parenthood, career, and contributing to society. The strength of generativity is learned if a person has found meaning in their roles of being a friend, parent, professional, and volunteer.

If a person feels stuck in her marriage, not connected with her children, and works in a dead-end job, the strength of generativity will not be acquired and she will experience stagnation. For some adults, a mid-life crisis will occur and they will look for intimacy and identity in another life partner. They also might try to re-learn the strengths of initiative and industry and find a new line of work to finish out their professional careers.

The last stage is integrity vs. despair occurs during the retirement years. The adult is faced with looking back and seeing if her life has meaning and integrity or anguish and despair. A person with integrity feels satisfied with her life, death is not feared, and even if all her dreams are not fulfilled, she still feels she lived her life with dignity and love.

Integrity embodies the fruit of the previous seven stages. If a person failed to gain the strengths of the earlier stages, he will be more likely to experience despair. It will be harder to successfully bring closure to his life because there will be regret over missed opportunities. He will most probably feel his life did not have much meaning.

Like a person's developing personality is complex, a newly formed complex clay sculpture requires a cast or braces to hold it in place while it is forming and solidifying. The clay sculpture also needs to be placed in the fire and be baked to further solidify it into the form it was created. Only after being baked is it strong enough to stand on its own without support.

In the same way, a person has to have acquired the positive human strengths of each stage of life to be able to let go of the "cast or braces," lean into the unknown, embrace her Divine Self, and practice living the prayer, "Thy will be done." A person has to persevere through her own hellish "fires" and learn she can trust the world, resolve conflicts, and gain meaning through suffering. Each time she is successful through this process, she is more likely to trust her Divine Self, trust her human strengths, and spiral upward to a more "heavenly" life. This occurs when you create a divine union between your human nature and your spiritual nature.

What would a person's life look like if he or she did not successfully complete any of the stages and did not gain healthy strengths? The person will not *trust* the world, so he will probably be in an unfulfilling relationship or not be able to sustain intimate relationships. The person will not be *autonomous* from her unhealthy family of origin issues, and will carry on with a dysfunctional way of interacting in the world. The person will not feel capable of taking the *initiative* and apply for better paying positions or seek healthier relationships. Since the person's *identity* will be negative or unknown, he or she will lead a frustrated life. A male will probably turn this into anger against the world. A female will probably turn the negative feeling inward and become depressed. A person who cannot gain *intimate* relationships will feel lonely, hurt, mad, and depressed. A person who is stuck in his marriage, estranged from his children, working at a dead-end job, and not feeling a sense of *generativity,* will feel negative, and soon fall into a state of *despair.*

Such people will not be able to stand the rigors of self-exploration, trust a Higher Power for guidance, and know that joy and happiness resides on the other side of suffering. They will become resentful of the "braces" or the "cast" that is trying to hold them together. They will remain stuck in an unhealthy human existence and not be able to know their Divine Self to help them through their journeys.

CHAPTER FIFTEEN

Trust vs. Mistrust

The early parent-child relationship is critical to the child's development. What children learn from their primary caregivers will be generalized to every other relationship.

If a child learns her parents will be there in times of need, she will acquire the strength of trust. She will then be more likely to trust herself, peers, authority figures, and her God.

If a child's primary caregivers were rejecting, indifferent, abusive, and showed erratic behavior, he will learn to mistrust his world. This will be generalized to not trusting himself. He will be less likely to trust his decision-making processes. He will not trust that others will like him. He won't trust that his schoolwork or art creations are worthy of praise.

At a young age, children deify their parents. Since children rely totally on their parents for their existence, they raise the parents to the level of a god. At an unaware level, children will revere their parents as gods. If the child learns the parents are untrustworthy, hostile, and unfair, unconsciously the child will generalize this to a Higher Being.

Ask yourself to name the top three traits of your God. If your list includes traits like judgmental, distant, or unfair, it is highly likely that you learned this about your parents from an early age. If your list includes traits like loving, caring, and forgiving, it is highly likely that your parents or other important people in your life taught you these world views by actions or discussions.

Some children were raised in a toxic environment along with their brothers and sisters, but beat the odds and grew up to be healthy and functional adults. The siblings grew up consistent with their poisonous upbringing. As adults, they don't have healthy strengths, are in unhealthy relationships, and are not growing and healing.

Why were their paths not the same? Research shows there are many dynamics that cause this to occur. One of the top reasons is that a healthy adult entered the child's life. A grandparent, an aunt or uncle, a coach, or a neighbor developed a healthy relationship with the child. In a safe environment, he or she taught and modeled to the child that he can trust his world. Another important reason may be the child had a higher than average intelligence. This helps the child to figure things out and realize the root of the family problems lie with the parents. The child learns to keep the toxic environment at bay and not internalize the troubles.

Sometimes an adult will have an insight that she is on the mistrust side of the trust continuum, or has way too much trust, which gets her into trouble. This insight is important, but how does she start the process of developing a healthy level of trust? She will need to find a trustworthy person to help "re-parent" her on this issue. This is tricky, because if she has learned to not trust people, who can she trust to help her acquire this needed strength? Usually a professional is needed to start this process. Many adults find a licensed counselor or social worker, or a minister or rabbi to talk with about this issue. Within this relationship, she will feel safer to share the hurtful things that have happened to her. When the professional hears her life story, respects her, feels empathy for her life difficulties, doesn't reject her, is willing to work with her, she will more likely learn to trust this person.

When the professional feels a trusting relationship is being created, he might ask the client who in her life she feels she could trust a little bit. A therapeutic homework assignment might be given to the client for her to take a calculated risk and ask that person to do some social activity together. The client will be challenged to use her "antenna" to monitor if the person is being trustworthy. If so, the client will consciously start trusting the person more and see if a healthy friendship can be created.

People who have not acquired a healthy level of trust tend to wear "glasses of mistrust." In contrast, people who have acquired the ego strength of trust wear "glasses of trust." For example, if a friend backs out of a social event at the last moment, the person with mistrust "glasses" is more likely to judge him as untrustworthy and will be less likely to include him again. The person with trust "glasses" is more likely to discern that his friend is legitimately overwhelmed at work and is staying late to catch up. He will wish him well, and include him in future activities.

Every situation in life is open to a variety of interpretations. In effect, there is no reality outside our interpretation of it. We create our own understanding and truths. We create our own reality. Is the glass half empty or half full? Is our friend backing out of a social engagement or does he really have to work into the evening? The trust "glasses" we wear will determine our answer to these questions. What glasses do you tend to wear more often? Do you tend to trust others or are you more skeptical and mistrust the motivations of others? Do you overly trust people and end up getting hurt?

Awareness of your position on the continuum of trust vs. mistrust is critical. This knowing of your propensities can motivate you to seek understanding and assistance. With this guidance you can "re-parent" yourself and start the process of gaining the functional and necessary strength of appropriate trust.

I had once seen a client three or four times. Not much progress was being made in our counseling sessions. I asked the woman to remember her nighttime dreams, record them, and bring them into my office so we could talk about them.

She returned the following week with this dream: a man was trying to break into her house. She was aware this was happening, and didn't know what to do. She was not overly fearful, but she didn't think she wanted this man in her house.

We talked about who this man could be. Metaphorically, was this her inner masculine that needed to be incorporated into her life? Was this her ex-husband who she wanted to return to her? These answers did not resonate with her. I asked if that man was me. Was the counseling process at a point where she was contemplating sharing deeper issues but she didn't know if she could trust me and let me in her "house?"

She smiled, nodded her head, and agreed that was the meaning of her dream. We talked about our relationship and the issue of trust. With time, trust was developed and we continued on with her therapeutic work.

A person who has acquired the strength of trust is more likely to live in the present moment and trust her life circumstances. She may mentally drift back in time and re-live a painful or pleasurable experience, but she will come back to the present moment and trust that goodness will prevail. She will plan for the future and learn from the past, and she will come back to the present moment to take the proper action.

An adult who trusts the world will be more likely to trust her Higher Being and acknowledge her human strengths, and create a divine union with her Divine Self. Paradoxically, the human strength of trust will allow her to see this strength as a gift from God. She will not have a need to maintain an ego, which will allow her to live *in* the world but not be *of* the world.

Take as long as you need to gain the awareness of where you think you lie on the continuum of the strength of trust vs. mistrust. Place a half inch to three quarter inch oval on the continuum and write the date above it.

Mistrust		Trust
Think	Feel	Act
1. Do you think you trust yourself to make the right decisions?	1. How do you feel around a person who has always treated you fairly?	1. When a person interacts with you, do you naturally stay with them or try to walk away?
2. Initially, do you think you trust or mistrust others?	2. Do you feel like you could trust this person more?	2. Do you sit alone at lunch or join others?

3. If you initially mistrust others, why do you think you do this?

3. How emotionally safe do you feel with your life-partner?

3. Would you take a risk and talk with your life-partner about the level of trust in your relationship?

Action Plan

1. Write down the name of one person you feel is most vital to your success at work. Next to that name, write two specific ways to build greater trust with that person. Over the next several days, seek out that person and initiate a discussion about trust. Find out how trustworthy he/she feels you've been and what, precisely, the two of you could do to increase and maintain greater trust.

2. For one week, sit quietly in your favorite chair, listen deeply, get out of your head and into your heart, and write about your experience.

3. Take a calculated risk and talk with your life-partner about the level of trust in your relationship.

CHAPTER SIXTEEN

The next three stages: Autonomy vs. Shame and Doubt, Initiative vs. Guilt, and Industry vs. Inferiority

These three stages are closely linked and build upon each other. If the human strength of autonomy is acquired, the strength of initiative will most likely be gained, which will greatly increase the likelihood that industry will be acquired. The opposite is also true. If a child does not acquire autonomy, but acquires shame and doubt, this will most likely lead to a lack of initiative, which will lead to not being industrious.

If a child's early environment is enriched by the parent reading to the child, reinforcing exploration, putting breakable items away, and celebrating first words, then the strength of autonomy is likely to be acquired.

In healthy environments, boundaries are set by the parents and caregivers. The child is given appropriate consequences for acts of defiance. The child has to ask permission to go outside. Acts of aggression will automatically get the child a time-out. Touching a hot stove or falling off a bike will also teach the child limitations. These effective parenting strategies and life experiences will help develop a healthy sense of shame and doubt. This will lead to the most functional level of development for the strength of autonomy.

When the child learns the house rules and gains confidence in her abilities to interact in that world, she will likely take the initiative and play well with others. She will likely have a good imagination and also play well by herself.

These human strengths will be taken into the elementary school years. The child will probably do well in school, have friends, join extracurricular activities, and gain a sense of industry.

As a young adult, he will feel he has the abilities to apply for a good job. He might volunteer and be a Big Brother for an underprivileged child. He will be more likely to take the initiative and ask an outstanding person for a date.

As a parent, this person will be less likely to try to live his life through his child. Having gained a healthy sense of autonomy, he will not try to live his unfulfilled dreams through his child. The parent will expose his child to different activities, and see where the child naturally excels and feels good about the activity. Even if the parent never achieved his goal of being a first-string high school football player, he will not unconsciously try to have his child fill that void for him.

Every child is born with a drive toward being autonomous. The abilities to walk and talk enable the child to motor away and say "no" to parents. As teenagers, this drive kicks in at a high level. Teens want to stay out later than their curfews, and show their autonomy by breaking the rules set by their parents.

Adolescents turn sixteen and cannot only walk away from parents, but also drive away. Teens' primary social groups are no longer their families, but their peer groups. Adolescents may work part-time, earn their own money, and buy food, clothes, and music to their own liking—and their parents' dismay.

Parents know this is normal and, to varying degrees, celebrate their teens drive toward autonomy so someday the older children will successfully move to independent housing. How this process occurs is the most important element.

If parents are overwhelmed, have mental health issues, or do not have sufficient resources (money, extended family, supportive friends), the process of their children striving for autonomy could become negative. The children's actions toward autonomy are taken as a personal affront.

A parent then might shout, use hurtful language, or even use physical force to block a child's normal attempts to exercise their autonomy.

When the child acquires shame and doubt, he probably will not be as industrious in school because his self concept will be negative, and one of inferiority. He will feel he doesn't have the initiative to read well, or learn basic math skills. An absent or laissez-faire parent will also cause these deficits. If there is not a significant change of environment or intervention, these deficits will be carried forward to adolescence and adulthood.

A man who acquired shame and doubt, guilt, and inferiority during his childhood, is likely to be underemployed. He is less likely to feel qualified to apply for a job that is higher up the chain of command. He is more likely to be in an unfulfilling relationship because he doesn't feel good about himself and never learned how to "play well with others." Even if he married a woman with healthy strengths, he probably will be resentful because he doesn't want his life partner "mothering" him. A woman with these deficits might find a man who presents himself as strong and able to protect her. But sometimes these "strong" characteristics are not healthy strengths, and ultimately he becomes abusive toward her.

John Donne penned, "No man is an island." All of us need to be connected with the continent of humanity. Autonomy does not mean you do not need anybody. It is not pushing people away or staying away from others. It is being your own person and using your God-given strengths and talents. It is being connected to others but not being enmeshed and not losing who you are. It allows you to ask for feedback and others' opinions, but making your own decisions. It is paradoxically being separate while you are part of a group.

Life becomes very difficult for people without the ego strengths of autonomy, initiative, and industry. Self-medicating through alcohol and drug use is common. Zoning out through watching excessive amounts of television is an escape mechanism. Complaining, being grumpy, irritable, and playing the role of victim are all possible ways of living in the world if one has these deficits.

How does such a person break this cycle or simply grow in this area? Like the previous stage, he needs to find a trusting relationship where these issues can safely be explored. Finding someone who will reflect your good traits to you is helpful. The professional or trusted friend will reflect the good traits she sees in the client/friend. A more positive self-concept will start to form. Shame and doubt beliefs will lose their power. Feelings of autonomy and an attitude of "I can do it" will be more conscious.

Taking the initiative and a small, calculated risk somewhere in your life is a good start. Apply for a better paying job, ask a person you like to have coffee together, or try an extracurricular activity that has always interested you. These activities will get you outside your small box and help you see that you can create successes and a bigger life.

Do you feel like it's been a while since you've taken the initiative in your professional life and the result is you feel stuck? Do you feel like your personal life is thriving, or do you need to take the initiative and read a best seller, call a friend, find a new hobby, or exercise?

The sense of accomplishment creates a good feeling. Are you industrious enough at work or do you need to find a new project or a new line of work? Are you tired of being a couch potato at home? If so, will you be industrious and clean a room, start a garden, volunteer at a non-profit agency, or play with your children?

The children's book *The Little Engine That Could* is a classic example of incorporating these strengths into one's life. In the story, a train must climb a high mountain to deliver toys to the children on the other side. As hard as the train tried, it could not make the tall climb. The train asked many big engines for help, but for a variety of reasons, they all declined. Finally, a little steam engine agreed to help. Slowly the cars began to move. As they climbed the steep hill, the little engine said over and over, "I think I can! I think I can!" Against all odds, the little engine was successful in helping the train get the toys to the children.

The belief "I think I can! I think I can!" comes from healthy strengths of autonomy, initiative, and industry. Learning how to tell time, add and subtract, read sentences, and use words to resolve conflicts instead of hitting, are not easy endeavors. With proper strengths, a child will think he can do it. Even if he initially fails, he will try again, and soon become more competent. This will continue into adulthood where he will more likely find a job that matches his skills, have good friends, be in a loving long-term relationship, and know he can handle, by himself or with the assistance of others, whatever crosses his path.

A person who has gained these strengths will believe he can handle whatever crosses his path. He knows he can resolve the problem or find someone who can assist. He remembers what worked or didn't work in the past, he sees how the possible solution might play out in the future, and comes back to the present moment to resolve the problem.

An adult who has these healthy strengths will not be over confident. He knows his strengths and his limitations. He has learned that hard work is important but he knows there is a bigger picture where God puts people in his life at the right time for assistance. He has learned autonomy so he can take the journey home to be one with God. He has learned initiative so he can do God's work on earth. He has learned industry so he can be diligent in his practices of creating a divine union with his Divine Self. Paradoxically, these human strengths will allow him to see this strength as a gift from God. He will not have a need to maintain an ego which will allow him to live *in* the world but not be *of* the world.

Take as long as you need to gain the awareness of where you think you lie on the continuums of the ego strengths of autonomy vs. shame and doubt, initiative vs. guilt, and industry vs. inferiority. Place a half inch to three quarter inch oval on each continuum and write the date above it.

Shame & Doubt	Autonomy
Guilt	Initiative
Inferiority	Industry

Think	Feel	Act
1. Do you think you can get your boss' job someday?	1. How does it feel to take a calculated risk?	1. Do you self-motivate at work or, do you wait for your boss to give you directions?

2. Do you think you're a Little Engine That Could?

2. Do you feel like you're a Little Engine That Could?

2. Do you act as if you are a Little Engine that Could?

3. Do you think you can accomplish more at work?

3. How does it feel to stay in your current relationship or job?

3. Do you take risks or stay on the beaten path?

Action Plan

1. Name three strengths of yours. Think about this during the week and name three more.
2. Utilize one of these strengths this week at work. If it is not in your job description, share with your boss how you would like to utilize this talent in a very specific way.
3. Take a calculated risk this week which will help you grow as a person.

CHAPTER SEVENTEEN

Identity vs. Role Confusion

At every high school graduation party across the nation, adults will ask the teenagers similar questions. "What are you going to do?" "What will you be studying?" "What's your major?"

All of these questions are helping (or forcing) the teens to figure out their identity. Our culture believes that during adolescence, the human strength to be developed is identity. Teens need to discern their academic strengths. They need to discern how their natural talents can be turned into a profession. They need to figure out what they are looking for in a partner.

Identity, or self-concept, is a learned phenomenon. It starts early in childhood by what is mirrored to the child. Culturally, we tend to mirror different messages to little girls than we mirror to little boys. For example, "Susie, you look so cute in that pink dress." "Latisha, give the toy to your friend. Girls play nice with each other." "Sarah, I bet you take really good care of your brother and sister." These statements reflect identity messages of beauty, self-sacrifice, and care giving.

Little boys receive different messages. "Steven, big boys don't cry." "Adam, what sports do you play?" "Wow, Tyre! You look like you're a strong young man." These statements suggest and mirror to boys that they need to repress their emotions, they need to be strong, and they have more value if they participate in athletic activities.

Parents are the main source of what is being mirrored to each child. Each statement made by a parent gets deposited in the child's identity make-up. Every message cannot be positive and true to that child. Hopefully, more messages are positive and reflect the true strengths and talents of the child.

All messages are sent in verbal and non-verbal ways. "I love you," and hugs communicate acceptance and a child is a worthwhile person. Scornful looks and statements like, "You're always bothering me," can create a negative self-concept.

Parents working hard at their jobs and around the house are stating that a work ethic is part of their identity. Giving the children chores and family work sessions help give the children similar identities.

Parents want their children to grow up to be successful. They want their children to be happy, find a loving life-partner, and make enough money to pay the bills and have a nice house. Sometimes messages are mirrored to children that are not mean-spirited, but which are not true to the child. For example, a high school senior might state to his dad and mom that he wants to be a teacher. His mom might respond that teachers don't make a lot of money. His dad might add that he always saw him as a businessman who climbs the corporate ladder and is really successful. These two messages make the teen's drive to teach World History, coach the tennis team, and be a healthy role model to adolescents, evaporate into thin air. The teen might take on the identity his dad reflected to him, struggle in college, and be unhappy in his entry level sales position. After a number of years of living this false identity, this person might figure out that it's okay for him to be a high school teacher.

If parents have not completed high school, do not read in front of their children, and do not push their children to succeed academically, an identity of a drop out may develop in a teenager. When parents yell at their children, ignore them, or generally do not reflect positive messages, role confusion may occur with the children and they will not see themselves as productive and valued members of society.

It is typical for teens to try on different identities during their adolescence. Within a four year period, a teen might try out for a sport because she might want the identity of a jock. The teen might try hard during practices, not experiment with drugs and alcohol, and try to please the coach. A couple of years later, she might want to try on the hat of a person who condemns the primary cultural values. She might smoke marijuana, and wear clothes made of hemp. She might denounce her parents' religious values and quit going to church. Later, she might join the drama club, die her hair black, talk about existential matters, and further retreat from her parents. Finally, she might be tired of never having any money, let her natural hair color grow back, apply for a job, buckle down to finish school, and re-join the friends she had during the athletic period of her life.

Is there a possibility you adopted an identity that is not right for you? In a broad sense, does your job energize you or does it rob you of energy? Do you find yourself often carried along as you are caught up in activities you enjoy at work? Or do you find yourself most often struggling against the current? During your free time, have you found a hobby where you exercise a natural talent that is not utilized in your profession, or do you mostly watch television?

You can always change your identity. You can enroll in school to gain the credentials for a new profession. You can cut your hair or let it grow. You can join a club to meet others or learn more about a subject. You can change your eating habits or exercise. You can join Toastmasters and learn public speaking skills.

If you're tired of the identity of being a troublemaker, start today being a different person. Think of yourself as the new identity, experience the feeling(s) associated with that identity, and now start acting as if you are that new person. If you're tired of living the life that everyone else expects, start being your own person today. What does that new person do? Does that new person need training to accomplish what he wants? How does it feel creating this new person in your mind?

Forming an identity is not a once in a lifetime endeavor. The identity you chose as an eighteen year old is probably not your true identity as a thirty or forty year old. Look back to your childhood and see what activities energized you. If your parents are still alive, ask them what you said you wanted to be when you grew up. Most people knew themselves better as twelve year olds than as thirty year olds. You were born with certain gifts and talents. You naturally used them when you were young. Start the process of shedding identities that no longer work for you. Return home to your True Self.

A person who has gained the strength of identity is more comfortable in her own skin in each and every present moment. She is actively in search for the right job or has found the vocation or avocation that is good for her and which brings goodness to the world. If she experiences something outside her level of expertise, she does not become defensive, but communicates effectively that she will have to learn more about the certain subject or pass on the work request.

An adult who has taken risks and done the hard world of knowing herself will then know her true identity is a child of God. She will more likely acknowledge that her traits and talents are gifts from God and create a divine union with her Divine Self. Paradoxically, she will feel strong yet humble and will have less of a need to maintain an ego which will allow her to be *in* the world but not be *of* the world.

Take as long as you need to gain the awareness of where you think you lie on the continuum of the strength of identity vs. role confusion. Place a half inch to three-quarters inch oval on the continuum and write the date above it.

Role Confusion   Identity

Think	Feel	Act
1. Do you think you have the right identity for yourself?	1. Does it feel like you have the right identity for yourself?	1. While you're working at your job, are you energized?
2. What other identities do you think about for yourself?	2. How would it feel to stay in your present relationship or job?	2. Are you involved in any extracurricular activities that are energizing?
3. Name three of your top talents. Are you using them in your job?	3. How would it feel to change jobs or your relationship?	3. Would you join an activity that you enjoyed as a child or adolescent?

Action Plan

1. On a piece of paper, write a job(s) or profession(s) that you think would match your unique personality and God-given talents. Share this with your life-partner or good friend. Ask for feedback.
2. Start looking for this occupation.
3. Ask your Higher Being for guidance with this process

CHAPTER EIGHTEEN

Intimacy vs. Isolation

The time-span of adolescence changes in our culture. Fifty years ago, this stage ended around eighteen years old. With a more sophisticated society, which calls for more education, and tougher economic times which sometimes does not allow the teen or young adult to live on his or her own, this developmental period is changing again and is being stretched to 21-23 years old.

The next developmental stage after adolescence is young adulthood, or as Jeffrey Arnett of the University of Maryland coined, "Emerging Adulthood." This stage starts around 18/21 and goes to approximately age 25 to 28. Arnett found that this age group does not feel they have fully reached adulthood. His research found that three individualistic qualities of character were necessary to attain adulthood. They are accepting responsibility for one's self, making independent decisions, and becoming financially independent. For many young adults, this period stretches into the later twenties.

Erik Erikson wrote that the developmental human strength to be gained during this period is intimacy. The term intimacy means the ability to develop close and meaningful relationships with other people. For many people, this means marriage or a committed life-long relationship. This strength can also be achieved through close, personal friendships.

If a person was successful with the previous developmental stage and developed a secure identity, he or she is more likely to take a risk, love another person, and develop an intimate, committed relationship. The opposite of this is isolation, where a person who doesn't know himself very well can lack confidence and be fearful of relationships, or become self-centered and promiscuous and is unable to really commit himself to another person.

"To love is to risk not being loved in return. To hope is to risk pain. To try is to risk failure, but risk must be taken because the greatest hazard in life is to risk nothing." The first sentence of this anonymous quote speaks of the risk of extending yourself to another person. There is a direct relationship between one's capacity to love, and one's capacity to feel pain. Each end of the continuum widens when one loves another person. One must have well-formed human strengths to persevere through the more difficult times of any intimate relationship.

Forming a secure identity means the ability to be intimate with one self. This includes knowing and loving oneself. From this foundation, one is more likely to love and intimately know another person. Being intimate with oneself means knowing and accepting one's strengths and weaknesses. From this state of knowing, comes the deep understanding and acceptance of another person…warts and all. Intimate conversations are shared about these more private matters and innermost secrets.

The intimacy vs. isolation developmental stage is the first time where ego-oriented self centeredness is confronted. One has to incrementally let go of a self-centered perspective if he wants to share his life with another person. One has to incrementally let go of one's self-absorbed ego to share love and affection with another person. One has to take risks and let go of one's self-preserving lifestyle to share private and intimate parts of her life. One has to get beyond one's narcissistic ego to enter into a relationship where one will be taking care of another person.

This is the stage where a person will transform the love she received as a child and begin to love and care for others. If the child learned that she can trust the world, she will be more likely to love another. If she learned that she is autonomous, she is more likely to have functional boundaries and love another person in a healthy manner. Is she learned the strength of initiative, she is more likely to take the initiative and create healthy and loving relationships. If she developed a sense of industry, she will be more likely to do the typical work that is within every relationship. If she likes her identity, it is easier for her to like and love others.

Adult examples of when a child did not learn the strength of autonomy are Momma's boys and Daddy's girls. These adults bend to their mom's or dad's requests. They are still looking to their parents for approval. They share more intimate details of their lives with their mom/dad than they do to their adult partner. The woman can turn into a princess and expect their husband to do everything for them. The man can expect stringent sex roles from his female partner and demand all cleaning, laundry, and cooking be done by her. These adults are stuck and incapable of intimacy with a life-partner.

There are two ends of the relationship continuum. Each are unhealthy and do not serve the person well. One end is the avoidant person. He has many fears. One of them is the fear of rejection. Since rejection is always a possibility and it always hurts, he feels it's better to play it safe and not get emotionally involved. Another one is the fear of a person losing himself. If his human strength of identity is not strong, he might feel that he cannot enter into a relationship because the other person might engulf him. He thinks he will lose the little bit of personal power he has, so he stays distant. The next is fear of commitment or putting off commitment. "I'll get married when I get a better job." Or, "I'll commit to you when we have more money." This fear can evolve from a dysfunctional childhood where a person learned that people who love you will hurt you. This also evolves from not trusting one's internal strengths, so one looks toward external things, like work and money, which one thinks will make or break the relationship.

The other end of the continuum is the dependent personality. Without strong human strengths and a sense of self, this person has a huge fear of separation. "Without another, who am I?" is her existential question. To keep another person in her life, she exhibits clinging behavior, tries at almost any expense to please her partner, and is needy and passive. She feels helpless and needs constant reassurance. She has an inability to start projects, tends to be naïve, and avoids disagreements and conflicts. Sadly, she tends to be submissive, and is sometimes willing to tolerate mistreatment and abuse from others.

Most people are somewhere in between these two extreme positions. In healthy relationships, sometimes you need someone to lean on. And other times you want to be independent and do things on your own. Sometimes it feels good to retreat from others and have your alone time. Other times it feels good to interact and be part of a group. It feels good to take care of others. And, it also feels good when someone takes care of you.

Projection is another dynamic that will deter you from creating intimate relationships. Projection is attributing unconscious attitudes or behaviors to another. Projection is how we create the world we see and participate. There is an old adage; "We do not see things as they are, but we see things as we are." Our prejudices and previous experiences of situations create our reality. For example, if you had a previous girlfriend who cheated on you, you will have a tendency to think your current girlfriend is cheating on you. Or, if you really wanted to make the high school cheerleading squad but did not, you might project this importance onto your daughter.

Christian mystic Thomas Merton said, "The beginning of love is to let those we love be perfectly themselves, and not to twist them to fit our own image. Otherwise we love only the reflection of ourselves we find in them." Do you think you are projecting some of your old attitudes and experiences onto your loved ones? If you let go of some of those projections, do you think a more intimate relationship will evolve? Do you feel your life-partner is projecting onto you? Would you communicate this to him or her?

When you walk through the aisles of any bookstores, there is always a huge section of self-help books on relationships, marriages, and how to relate to one another. The demand for these books is high because many people do not know how to develop the strength of intimacy in a healthy manner. One of the biggest problems is that teens, young adults, and adults equate having a sexual relationship with intimacy. They think being physically intimate creates an intimate relationship. This is not true; in fact, many people feel extremely alone and isolated after being sexual active.

The foundation of any intimate relationship is not sex, but an emotional component. Trust is the building block of all emotional relationships. From a trusting foundation sprouts a strong friendship that includes mutual respect, understanding and acceptance of the other person's strengths and weaknesses. A kinship develops, communication flourishes, and the uneasy process of resolving conflicts are resolved because of the commitment to the relationship. The couple has similar interests, affection is strong, and the care giving is reciprocal.

Erik Erikson defined intimacy as "finding oneself yet losing oneself to another." This will occur when two independent people want to create something larger than themselves. This is more likely to occur when the person is strong and more fully developed. The mature person can transcend the differences in the sexes, the differences in personalities, the differences of opinions, and resolve the natural antagonisms that are involved in all relationships.

"Love me when I least deserve it, because that's when I really need it," is a Swedish proverb that speaks to getting outside of yourself, and loving another. Do you already see yourself doing this, or do you need to be more aware of your selfishness and practice more fully loving another person? Do you believe you are practicing the Thomas Merton quote and "let(ting) those we love be perfectly themselves?" or are you projecting your needs onto them?

A person who has developed the strength of intimacy doesn't live in the past and wish for lost relationships or doesn't live in the future waiting for the perfect partner. He lives in the present moment and loves God. He loves himself with all of his strengths and weaknesses and loves others the same way.

An adult who forms intimate relationship be more likely to form an intimate relationship with God and create a divine union with his Divine Self. Paradoxically, this human strength of intimacy will allow him to see this strength as a gift from God. He will be less likely to have a need to maintain an ego which will allow him to live *in* the world but not be *of* the world.

Take as long as you need to gain the awareness of where you think you lie on the continuum of the ego strength of intimacy vs. isolation. Place a half inch to three-quarter inch oval on the continuum and write the date above it.

Isolation		Intimacy
<u>Think</u>	<u>Feel</u>	<u>Act</u>
1. Do you think you are involved in an intimate relationship?	1. Do you feel you are involved in an intimate relationship?	1. How do you respond when someone wants to be emotionally closer to you?
2. Do you think you are willing "to love (and) risk not being loved in return?"	2. Do you feel a connection with others or do you feel distant?	2. Do you share private matters with someone you trust?
3. What is holding you up from entering into an intimate relationship?	3. Do you feel like it is time to let go of a hurt ego and love someone?	3. What would you do to more fully create a mutually satisfying relationship?

Action Plan

1. Take a calculated risk and let someone you trust more fully into your life.
2. Resolve a conflict with your life partner or someone you're close to.
3. Act "as if" you more fully trust someone and create a more intimate friendship.

CHAPTER NINETEEN

Generativity vs. Stagnation

The middle adult years are the longest developmental stage. This stage begins approximately in the mid to late twenties, and generally ends in the mid to late sixties when a person retires from his or her work.

The human strength of generativity comes from finding meaning in one's life. Successfully raising children, making contributions at work, and contributing to society, are the main sources of building the strength of generativity. It comes from being creative and productive in the many different dimensions of one's life. It is also created by enjoying family, friends, and work.

Since some adults do not have children, generativity involves more than parenthood. Adults want to bring benefit to others and help future generations. Volunteering at non-profit organizations, mentoring youth, coaching athletic teams, and cleaning up the environment, are examples of teaching one's values, maintaining and enhancing one's culture.

Successfully navigating through the previous two stages is imperative. Knowing yourself and finding your true identity is necessary so you will find the right occupation and be able to use your innate strengths and talents. The strength of generativity will be developed when contributions are made to society suitable to your particular potential.

Being able to be intimate with a life-partner, maintain a marriage while persevering through the stress of raising children is essential to raise emotionally healthy children. Transmitting your values and raising self-reliant children is an important part of gaining the ego strength of generativity. If you don't have children, being involved in the lives of your nephews and nieces, mentoring a child who is at-risk for unhealthy behaviors, or coaching a youth athletic team, are important dynamics of gaining generativity.

It is necessary and imperative to get outside of one's self to successfully gain the strength of generativity. If a person is going to be a healthy and functional parent, spouse, volunteer, and employee, he must think of others and help others. He will not take advantage of others or harm them...including himself. This paradigm will create win-win situations.

A person stuck in himself might help another person but will do so in unhealthy ways. He might help another quid pro quo; he will be helpful only if the other person will do something for him. Another way could be through trying to live through another person. For example, a dad who drives his son to football practices, buys him the best equipment, and roots him on at every game. His unconscious motivation is to fill a void in him that is there because he was not successful at football during his playing days as a youth. His son might not enjoy football but dad doesn't acknowledge this because he is blinded by his ambitions.

Being motivated to volunteer at a non-profit or helping to raise funds for a worthy cause because you want to be seen by others as a "good person" is another unhealthy example. This might create a bloated ego that needs to be continually fed by others.

Working in a non-rewarding job is one of the reasons stagnation occurs. Doing mundane work, spending eight hours in a toxic environment, and not being able to use your talents will make you feel non-productive and unhappy.

Staying in a conflict-filled relationship with your life-partner is another reason stagnation occurs. Constantly quarreling and hurting each other is devitalizing. This type of marriage will certainly affect the relationship with your children. A home filled with tension and strife will strain all relationships. Children will retreat to their rooms or friends houses. Sometimes children pick sides and shun one parent. Divorce may cause a dad to only see his children on Wednesdays and every other weekend. This leaves moms economically poorer, overwhelmed, and not able to spend as much quality time with her children. All of these dynamics causes stagnation.

Middle age crisis occurs during this stage. This is more likely to occur to adults who have not examined their lives. Typically, a man reaches forty to fifty years old, is unhappy with his marriage, does not have a close relationship with his children, and is not fulfilled at work. He realizes his youth has passed and old age is imminent. He might have remorse for goals not accomplished. He questions decisions made in earlier years, and has undefined goals for his future.

This person is cynical, rejects himself and others, and stuck in stagnation. He does not look inside for an answer to his unhappiness, but looks outside for happiness in a younger woman, alcohol, and gets involved in conspicuous consumption. He thinks he will find meaning and purpose in these external things. In time, these coping strategies will likely make him more depressed.

Kevin Spacey's character, Lester Burnham, in the 1999 drama *American Beauty*, is a quintessential male experiencing a mid-life crisis. He states, "I'm 42 years old. In less than a year I'll be dead. And in a way, I'm dead already." He states this because his marriage is in shambles, he works in a dead-end job for a boss who he doesn't respect, and has an unhappy daughter.

The way Burnham deals with these crises is to look outside of himself for happiness. He quits his job to escape the stress, he becomes infatuated with his daughter's friend, works out to impress her, buys his dream car; a 1970 Pontiac Firebird, and starts smoking marijuana. These coping strategies resolve nothing in his life, and he ends up getting killed.

Edward Guthman of the San Francisco Chronicle wrote of the movie, "It is a dazzling tale of loneliness, desire, and the hollowness of conformity." Sadly, too many adults in this stage of life find themselves in this state. They have not looked inward and examined their lives. They bury their heads in the sand and have not resolved the typical conflicts that occur with families and work. They have not taken calculated risks and looked for jobs that are better fits for their personalities. They have not got outside of themselves and more fully developed their spiritual lives.

The culture in which we live has values and standards that help guide the decisions we make about our lives. We can become stuck in this stage of life if we do not examine these cultural mores. For example, living the "American Dream" includes the freedom to pursue goals through hard work and free choice. The goal of working hard has turned out to mean "keeping up with the Joneses," buying bigger homes, and buying the latest fashions and electronic devices. This norm lures us to stay in jobs that we don't like, spend money we don't have, and impress people we don't even know. This endless cycle of the rat of the treadmill does not lead us anywhere. We become tired, disgruntled, and stagnated.

Many people are governed by "shoulds." "I should work hard." "I should enroll my kids in many activities." "I should earn more money so I can buy better things for my family." These "shoulds" are usually sticks that we pick up and beat ourselves with. Where did these "shoulds" come from? Do I need to live my life by these "shoulds?"

Socrates said, "An unexamined life is not worth living." Start the process of exploring your life and come to your own conclusions about how you want to live your life. Are you on a treadmill that is taking you nowhere? Are you picking up a "should" stick and beating yourself? Are you too busy to spend quality time with your spouse and/or children? Are you resisting some difficult choices that could lead you to freedom? What makes you happy? What legacy do you want to create? When you near the end of your life, do you think you'll state, "I wish I would have worked more hours at my job?"

Western culture also has a value of redemption. Movies and books often portray a character who experienced negative events in his life. This person worked hard, pulled himself up by the bootstraps, and turned his life around. We love the underdog who fights the odds and, in the end, wins the event. We make bumper stickers that say "Make Lemonade out of Lemons."

Religion is redemptive, and the Judeo-Christian faiths have many stories of atonement, salvation, and deliverance from sin. Many people believe that the debt of their mistakes against them is not viewed as simply cancelled but it is fully paid. These stories instill hope and help us continue on with our journeys toward more meaningful lives.

An honest and frank appraisal is useful in figuring out a new course in life. Because confrontation with one's own mortality is real during this stage, everything needs to be re-examined. Some of the things we thought were so important give way to much larger and more important dimensions. Working long hours so to buy the latest gadgets gives way to solitude and finding inner peace. Giving yourself endlessly to your children and grandchildren gives way to long forgotten creative ventures.

Sigmund Freud believed that the two foundations for a happy and healthy life are the abilities to work and love well. One cannot escape the ambivalent feelings that are involved in any work and love relationship: parent-child, spouse-spouse, and boss-employee. For example, parents feel joy around their children, and also feel anger when the children don't obey. A worker may feel appreciation when a boss helps him, and also feel resentment when the boss makes him work overtime. A wife may feel thankful when her husband helps around the house, and also feel irritated when he plays golf with his buddies.

The emotionally and mentally mature person can hold both of these paradoxical feelings. The well developed person can embrace both-and thinking. The parent feels *both* joy *and* anger. The worker feels *both* appreciation *and* resentment. The wife feels *both* thankful *and* irritated. The emotionally and mentally underdeveloped person thinks in a dualistic manner. This parent holds on to anger and is less likely to find the joy in any activity with the child. The worker only remembers the resentment, so he is less likely to feel any appreciation. And the wife holds on to being irritable so she doesn't feel appreciation toward her husband.

The person with healthy and functional strengths is able to rise above the disparate emotions and move forward being a successful employee, spouse, volunteer, and parent. This person will persist through the difficult times and successfully fulfill his duties. He will not get stuck in the inevitable conflicts that arise. He will have the necessary strengths to resolve the conflict and paradoxically, use the conflict to cultivate an even stronger relationship.

A person who has gained the strength of generativity is comfortable with his past and does not fear the future. He lives in the present moment and actively shares herself with others.

Adults who gained the human strength of generativity have successfully, to varying degrees, learned that they can't be self absorbed and life is not all about them. To be in life means getting outside of one's self. They are better able to generate heaven on earth. Paradoxically, this human strength of generativity will allow people to see their strengths as gifts from God. They will not have a need to maintain their egos which will allow them to live *in* the world but not be *of* the world.

Take as long as you need to gain the awareness of where you think you lie on the continuum of the ego strength of generativity vs. stagnation. Place a half inch to three-quarter inch oval on the continuum and write the date above it.

Stagnation   Generativity

<u>Think</u>	<u>Feel</u>	<u>Act</u>
1. Do you think you find meaning in your life?	1. Do you feel like you find meaning in your life?	1. How do you react on Sunday night when you realize work is tomorrow?
2. Do you think you are making contributions to a better society?	2. Do you feel like you are making contributions to a better society?	2. Do you look for happiness in external things are more internal ways?
3. Do you think your life life is governed by "shoulds?"	3. Do you feel happy most of the time?	3. Do you have goals for your future?

Action Plan

1. Write your obituary. Do you like what it says?
2. Make one change in your marriage that will help vitalize it.
3. Write someone a note or call them on the phone and let him or her know how thankful you are for the friendship.

CHAPTER TWENTY

Integrity vs. Despair

One's social roles may be changed rather dramatically during the last Eriksonian stage of development. A person in her retirement years will probably not get up in the morning and go to work. She will not be raising children at home. Friends may have recently died or a spouse might have a life threatening illness.

How does one respond to not contributing at work anymore? How does one feel about the work one has done for the last forty years? How does a person in this stage feel about how her children turned out? Does she feel close to her adult children? Is she making a positive impact on her grandchildren?

How does one respond to the profound sense of mortality? Is he accepting or fearful of death? Does he help a friend through the process of dying or does he stay away? Does he practice healthy living habits or has he unconsciously given up on life?

How one responds to these questions will show if the strength of integrity or despair has been formed. While reviewing your life, some of the big questions are; "Am I happy with the way I lived my life?" and "Do I feel my life was generally a success or failure?"

A person with integrity views his life with satisfaction. His personality and life efforts are generally congruent with how he sees himself. Even though he experienced hard times and made his share of mistakes, he feels self-respect and forgives himself when he fell short.

He has made peace with himself, others, God, and the final passage of death. A person with integrity has wisdom. Erikson defined wisdom as an "informed and detached concern with life itself in the face of death itself."

A person with despair has a sense of dissatisfaction with his life. He has not resolved past mistakes and conflicts. In fact, he may be preoccupied with past events, lose interest in present day life, and be depressed. He has not come to terms with his life which means he can't come to terms with death. He feels life is unfair, too short, and he fears what lies ahead after death.

Erik Erikson wrote, "And it seems possible to further paraphrase the relation of adult integrity and infantile trust by saying that healthy children will not fear life if their elders have integrity enough not to fear death."

This quote shows the importance of successfully navigating through the eight developmental stages. Our lives are interconnected and the healthy acquisition of strengths has positive effects on others. The opposite is also true.

If you are before the age of retirement and have read the first eight chapters of this book, I hope you see life a little differently now and ask yourself some new questions so you will be more likely to land on integrity later in your life. Here are some of the questions that may help you re-focus and more fully stay on the road to integrity.

- Am I teaching important life skills to younger people?
- Am I making contributions to my community?
- Am I sharing important knowledge to others that has helped me in my life journey?
- Am I letting people know I love them?
- Am I creating intimate relationships where there is trust, mutual support, and we feel safe enough to challenge each other?
- Am I aware that my time on earth is finite and am I currently leaving a legacy?

- Do I take responsibility for the problems in my life or do I blame others?
- Do I make a positive impact on others?
- Do I need to make amends with another person?
- Am I growing in my spiritual development?
- Am I connected to my Divine Self?
- Do I feel free?